$TREET $MART NETWORK MARKETING

A No-Nonsense Guide for Creating the Most Richly Rewarding Lifestyle You Can Possibly Imagine

ROBERT BUTWIN

WITH CONTRIBUTIONS FROM RUSS DEVAN

PRIMA PUBLISHING

PRIMA PUBLISHING and colophon are registered trademarks of Prima Communications, Inc.

Library of Congress Cataloging-in-Publication Data

Butwin, Robert.
    Street smart network marketing : a no-nonsense guide for creating the most richly rewarding lifestyle you can possibly imagine / Robert Butwin.
          p.   cm.
    Includes bibliographical references and index.
    ISBN 0-7615-1000-1
    1. Multilevel marketing. I. Title.
    HF5415. 126.B875   1997
    658.8'4—dc21
    96-27234   CIP

    99 00 01 HH 10 9 8 7 6 5 4 3
Printed in the United States of America

How to Order
Single copies may be ordered from Prima Publishing, P.O. Box 1260BK, Rocklin, CA 95677; telephone (916) 632-4400. Quantity discounts are also available. On your letterhead, include information concerning the intended use of the books and the number of books you wish to purchase.

Visit us online at www.primapublishing.com

To my wife Bonnie for being patient when times were tough. She always knew, as I did, that one day, it would all be worth it. She was right.

Also to those people who have contributed their Street Smart knowledge to this book and to my life, but whom I did not specifically mention as my mentors—especially to Dick and Arlene Smith.

To Doris Wood of the MLMIA (Multi-Level Marketing International Association) for her inspiring leadership—and her friendship. To Russ DeVan, whose thoughtful and experienced contributions have enriched the book—and my life—immeasurably. And to John Milton Fogg and John David Mann, the good people of *Upline*™, who helped in so many ways to put this book together and bring it to you.

And finally, to you, for having the desire to become a Street Smart Networker. Now, go out there and *be great!*

Contents

Contents

Foreword

"Street Smart . . ." — good title! That term sums up exactly what's needed to build a solid MLM business.

This is no place for college-smarts or theoretical "here's-how-to's." This is a business for ordinary people—and I count myself, along with Robert Butwin and other esteemed colleagues, as among the ordinary people who have achieved *extraordinary* success, just as this book will help you to do as well. But too often, too many people, with resumés that boast all kinds of degrees and all kinds of success in other kinds of businesses, think they can breeze into Multi-Level Marketing and show us "dummies" how to do it.

And quite often, they fall flat on their noses.

MLM, a.k.a. Network Marketing, actually needs a unique "people-people" talent and a certain brand of common sense—unfortunately, all too uncommon in today's how-to self-help business books. Fortunately for all of us, Robert brings together both these abilities along with his hard-earned Street Smart knowledge, plus the advice of his many mentors, to make things easier both for the novice and the MLM Old Timer.

I especially like Robert's detailed instructions on how to use the phone to build a business. Here's a classic example of working Street Smart.

Most people *don't* have the time or money to travel, go to scores of meetings, or make in-person, one-on-one presentations every day. And, most people *can* work phone business-building into their lives. I've built my own business largely from my home, on the phone, wearing blue jeans (or whatever I felt like wearing on that particular day).

That's the way this business is supposed to work.

In fact, that's the way this business *does* work—as you're about to read.

Enjoy!

—Venus Andrecht,
author of *MLM Magic:*
How an Ordinary Person Can Build An
Extraordinary Networking Business From Scratch

Introduction

As I write this, I'm lounging by the pool here in Hawaii, talking with some friends about the book you now hold in your hands, and my friend and mentor Robert Natiuk asks me,

"Robert, why did you write this book? And who do you think will read your book?"

"Well," I tell him, "I wrote it as my way of giving back to others who are striving to achieve the lifestyle that we're able to live because of this business. I wanted to cover those points that were instrumental in us becoming successful—points that other books don't cover."

... And who will read it? I think about that for a minute. "Two types of people. People who are already successful Network Marketers, but they'll be the smaller group by far. They'll read the book to pick up a new tip or two, another way to explain some point to their people—things like that.

"Then there'll be all the new people looking for *how* to do the business, *how* to be successful."

And then Robert asks me, "What is it that you want those new people to know most?"

I think about that for a moment. It's a *good* question.

It wasn't all that long ago that I was a "new people" myself. What did I want to know most?

I wanted to know that the business *really could work for me.*

I didn't really care if it took a while to master the skills and insights required to succeed in Network Marketing. I just wanted to know—for sure and without a doubt—that the business could work for me if I made the commitment to work the business.

I looked around at the people who were making it in the industry. There were lots of them—*LOTS.* They were with different companies, representing different products, and most were approaching the business in different ways as well.

And the people themselves were all so very different. My friend Robert is a professional writer; his wife, a musician. There were sales people (like me) and people who'd never sold a thing in their lives—doctors, teachers, engineers, truck drivers, high school coaches, a bellhop, a motivational speaker, an insurance agent, a massage therapist . . . So many, many different experiences, educational backgrounds, and lifestyles—yet all of them had become successful in this business.

That's the one single fact that convinced me that I could do this business if I really wanted to—the fact that all of these people from different backgrounds were succeeding with different products and companies and compensation plans and trainings.

Look around. Look at all the tremendous success stories in our business and realize Network Marketing can succeed for you, too.

That's the magic of this wonderful business of ours. Everybody and anybody has an equal shot at success. You don't have to have any specific experience or preparation to begin. All you need to succeed is to get the knowledge of how the business works, then work it, and don't quit till it's time to retire.

This book will give you more than enough knowledge to

do really well in Network Marketing—if you work at it—and *keep* working at it.

That's what I've done and what I continue to do—work at it. And believe me, sitting here in the Hawaiian sun, sipping a cool drink, talking with my dear friends . . . this is *work*: Network Marketing—the greatest work in the world!

R.B.

CHAPTER ONE

What's Happening?

SO, WHAT'S "STREET SMART NETWORKING"?

Where I come from, somebody who's *street smart* is somebody who knows what's happening . . . who knows the ropes—knows where they're going, and how to get there. Somebody who is a *survivor*.

In Network Marketing, a *Street Smart Networker* is a man or woman who has a clear vision of the big picture, plus the common-sense "street smarts" to know how to play the game and win—and do it with integrity.

So, what's a Street Smart Networker?

Here's What's Happening for Street Smart Networkers . . .

Street Smart Networkers have main men and women—people who are their mentors, teachers, counselors and coaches.

Street Smart Networkers know where it's really at—they know the truth about themselves, about their business and about the industry.

Street Smart Networkers are into "getting the gold," big

1

time—they've got clear, stated (and *written*) goals that support their life's purpose *and* they've got a plan for getting them.

Street Smart Networkers know when to "Just Say No"— "No" to anything and everything that doesn't empower them or serve others.

Street Smart Networkers know and go where the action is—they *are* the action.

Street Smart Networkers have a "hot set of wheels"— they're driving the best vehicle for them, and by "vehicle" I mean both their company and the opportunity of Network Marketing itself.

Street Smart Networkers are always "Takin' Care of Business"—they're always learning, their attitude is "up" and they're focused on creating results.

Street Smart Networkers have "brothers" and "sisters"— they're part of a team of committed players. They're in partnership with all the men and women in their Network— downline *and* upline—and in the industry itself, too.

Street Smart Networkers are team leaders—they know leadership is where the power is, and they know what that power gives them. And, they know that the most awesome power of all is in empowering *others*.

Street Smart Networkers know "black belt MLM"—they know the success secrets—about using the right tools to do the work, about who to get on their team and how. Above all, they know all about *leverage*.

Street Smart Networkers love payday—they've played hard and worked hard; they've earned their rewards, and they know what to do with them. They know how to create balance in their lives, too. They've got their cake *AND* they're eating it!

Street Smart Networkers are free!

This book will take you through every one of these topics. But the most important one of all is that last one—"Street Smart Networkers are free!" That's what this book *and* this business are all about.

Being free is the *why* of all the how-to's. It's the goal you need to connect with right up front. And understand what I mean by "goal": It's not only the *reward* you get for building your successful Network Marketing business and doing it right. Truth is, freedom is also the journey of getting there. And that's so important because, as the saying goes, "The road to success is always under construction."

Network Marketing *IS* the Freedom business. *Get that*— and you've got it all.

Street Smart is a way of being. When you're *being* Street Smart, you're free because you know you always have a choice. You don't *have to* do anything. What you do, you choose to do. It more than *feels* right. It's the best choice of all.

All Things To All People

Okay, so if you're a Street Smart Networker, what are you?

Sometimes, you're a street fighter—You're tough as nails, you're the one who throws the first punch; you're a wall and nothing gets by you.

Sometimes, you run—You get out, move on! When you see something isn't working, you quit doing it and do something different. And, you do it better.

Sometimes, you're the "old man" or "old lady" the kids come to for advice—You've been around, you've got wisdom; they need attention and they know you care and can be counted on.

Sometimes you're the big brother or sister—You stand up for them, step in, make it safe, show them how it's done.

Sometimes you even do it for them—but not for long.

Sometimes you're smoke—You're moving so fast the only clear thing you see is what's dead ahead—everything else is just a blur!

Sometimes you watch and wait—You know timing is everything. You never waste time—you're a doer, not a reactor.

Sometimes you're the star . . . other times, the star-maker—Sometimes you take center stage; other times, you hang back, push other people up front. Once in a while, one of your people doesn't have the courage it takes to stand up front, so you go with them, be up there next to them, ease them into it. Once they get cooking, you split—and they don't even know you're gone till they see you standing there, cheering for them out in front with the others.

Sometimes you lead . . . sometimes you follow . . . and sometimes, you even *disappear!*—You know that sometimes the best way to lead is to get out of the way.

Sometimes, you're all those things—and *most times* you are one on-purpose machine! "Takin' care of business" is what Elvis Presley used to say, and that's what Street Smart Networkers do every day. How do they do it? Whatever way it takes—and it takes all kinds of ways.

Doing It Your Way

Now, that's *something like* what a Street Smart Networker looks like.

But the truth is, you won't look exactly like that. I don't, and you won't either.

So what will you look like—exactly?

If you want to see what a Street Smart Networker *really* looks like, here's what you do:

Read this book; check out all the street-smart ways you can. Find out, for yourself, what works, and what doesn't. Do what works—and *don't* do what *doesn't* work (no matter *who* tells you to). Then ask the people you've taught and trained, the people you've helped become successful—what do they see when they look at you?

Then you'll know what *one* Street Smart Networker looks like—but *only* one—you. And there are many, many different kinds of Street Smart Networkers.

Network Marketing *is not* "Send in the Clones." No matter what I tell you—or what anybody else tells you— it's a Burger King business: "Do it your way."

My job with this book isn't to mold you into little Robert Butwins—and I hope you're as clear about that as I am.

My job *IS* to give you all the street smart know-how that it's taken me years to get—in just a couple of hours of your reading and thinking time.

My job is to give you all I've got about how to build a successful Network Marketing business while avoiding many of the rip-offs and dead ends that have tripped up others before you. You'll save your time and money, and your progress won't be slowed down by taking short cuts over cliffs! You can learn by the successes I'll tell you about—and maybe even more than that, from my mistakes.

And speaking of my mistakes, let's look for a minute at how to do it "Country Club Stupid."

The "Country Club Stupid" Networker

When I first got into this business, I wasn't street smart. I had the kind of smarts you get 23 stories up in a downtown office building. Looking out my 23rd-story window, looking for the "best deal ..." Big Deal is right. I was "Country Club Smart."

First thing I did was "get sponsored" by grabbing the first guy that hit on me with the first MLM company I heard about. I leased a fancy office—downtown and up high—with the "right" address. I placed ads in the newspaper aimed at the heavy hitters and needy-greedies. Hired a staff and wired in a bank of phones.

One year and more than $100,000 in expenses later, I hit the skids. Reach into your pockets and pull them inside out. That's what I looked like.

My sponsor was the invisible man. Never saw the guy again. The high-flying MLM company I signed up with got into a gang war with the FDA. That's another way of saying: They took on the cops. Guess who lost?

Poor Robert.

At that point, here's what I *had* that I *didn't want:*

> *... a big bunch of debt ... a failed first effort in Network Marketing ... a "straight" job in my parents' business that I was none too thrilled with ... a how-low-can-you-go self-image ... and clearly no idea of what I was doing—though I did have a great idea of what NOT to do!*

Now, here's what I *didn't have* that I *did want:*

> *... all the money to do all the things I wanted to do and get all the things I wanted to have.*

I didn't own my own time and life—I wasn't free.
I didn't have it yet, but I knew what I wanted: I wanted

a successful, full-time Network Marketing career.

And never ever, even for one minute, did I lose sight of that vision—in fact, I learned to put that vision on Center Stage.

Center Stage

I learned something early on from Dr. K. Dean Black:

Whatever you put center stage in your mind, magnifies itself.

Sure, you're going to have thoughts about what's not working, about all the mess-ups and snafu's and what's going wrong. But keep them off in the wings where they belong. Put your vision of success center stage, forward.

My first "Country Club Stupid" year in the business was the beginning of my "Get Smart" program. That's when I hit the streets to learn the ways of the Networking world.

I never lost the vision and I kept on learning. Those two things alone saved my skin and helped me make it through the night more than once—a lot more.

Now all those things that I *had and didn't want* are no longer part of my life.

And now, all those things I *wanted and didn't have*— I have!

Do you keep score with money? I do. Why? Because it's fun! I passed through the six-figure door a good ways back.

And that reminds me of a key point about being a Street Smart Networker—it's both a secret *about how to* "do it right," and a *benefit for* "doing it right." But not everyone knows about it . . . so here it is:

Street Smart Networkers are having a blast!

Big time fun is what this business and lifestyle are all about.

Now, all this good stuff happened for me because I learned how to be a Street Smart Networker—and that's what I'm going to show you now.

Ready to play?

Good—because it's game time!

What "game"?

It's the Network Marketing game, what some of us call *"The* Accelerated Game of Life"!

CHAPTER TWO

My Main Men and Women

I USED TO HAVE A TENDENCY TO SINK ALL MY OWN SHIPS.

Maybe you already know what this looks like: I'd become somewhat successful, just starting to make some decent money—and then, somehow, I'd find a way to sabotage myself. I didn't realize I was doing this. I just did it. And boy, was I good at it.

"There goes Robert. He can snatch defeat from the very jaws of victory!"

I needed to find a way to break that failure pattern.

Then somebody handed me a tape series by Dr. Wayne Dyer called "The No Limit Person." I listened to those tapes over and over and over; I nearly wore them out!

Here's what I saw about my own life from Dr. Dyer's tape set:

Without realizing that I was the one doing it, I had placed all kinds of limitations on myself—limitations that weren't true, didn't serve me, and weren't necessary!

9

In fact, most of us do this without even realizing that we're the ones doing it. That really opened my eyes and ears. That experience gave me an appetite to listen, to study and read whatever other successful people had available. And I approached that learning like a buffet lunch: I selected, tasted and, when I found something that resonated within me, I devoured it!

I realized that for me to become successful, I had to focus first on my own personal growth and development. In fact, the reason I'm telling you about this is that it's important for you to know that this really is the personal development business.

And that's why this next principle is so vital:

Street Smart Networkers have mentors.

Now, the word "mentor" means someone who is a trusted friend and advisor. People usually think of a mentor (or coach, teacher or guru) as someone who's right there with you, holding your hand, showing you the ropes strand by strand.

Not necessarily.

My first Network Marketing mentor *in the flesh* was Robert Natiuk—but before I ever met Robert, my *very* first mentor, Wayne Dyer, came out of a box! Never met the man. But he gave me an appetite for more. And he inspired me to seek out a real-live mentor.

In the rest of this chapter, I'm going to tell you a little about some of my mentors, for two reasons. First, I want to introduce you to who they are, what they've taught me and what they stand for. And second, I want to whet your appetite for going out and finding your own mentors!

It's the Street Smart thing to do.

Rudolph, let me get this straight: The only way you'll drive my sleigh tonight is if I make you front line to the company, and transfer Donner, Blitzen, Comet, Cupid and the other reindeer into your downline, AND kick back to you 80 percent of the commissions Mrs. Claus and I earn on you and your group?

It's Not About Doing Deals

Remember how I said that in the beginning, I was the guy looking for "the best deal"? So, what do you suppose was one of the first things I heard from my first real-live mentor, Robert Natiuk?

That's right—*no deals.*

"Robert," he would insist, "deals rarely if ever work."

Problem was, I didn't listen to him. Oh, I heard him all right—but I didn't *listen.*

For instance, I once met a guy named Pierre at a trade show where I had a Network Marketing booth. Pierre, who also had a booth at the same show, told me about this great direct mail piece he was able to get on a pro-rated basis. And, he said, he had a hot list! These names were just going to jump into my mail box and sign right up! Pierre said he'd join *my* opportunity if I'd put up $3,000 for *his* mail order program.

So, Country Club Stupid Robert smelled a real deal.

I put up the three grand, sat back and waited for cash to pour out of my mail box.

Nothing.

Natiuk was right. Pierre disappeared and I would have had to go to court to get my money back—and even then, there'd be a very slim chance of *that*. Besides, going to court is a pretty negative approach to building your business.

So, there's the difference between Street Smart and Country Club Stupid. I'd just spent three grand for a lesson my mentor had offered me *for free!* Expensive—but sometimes that's what it takes. Sure, it would have been cheaper to listen to my mentor. But I wasn't Street Smart—yet.

I continued to try lots of *deals* over the years. And sure enough, Natiuk was right. Rarely did any of them ever work. What I've learned is, if you make any deals, first clarify both parties' expectations, and make the deal conditional UPON RESULTS.

Now that I'm a mentor for other people, I tell them, "Deals rarely work." And some of them actually listen. You know, there really aren't any special deals as far as the road to success goes. Natiuk told me that, too.

Teach Your Children Well—And Don't Give Up

One purpose a mentor serves is to keep you from having to *reinvent the wheel*. Sometimes, though, mentors encounter stubborn pupils. I'm like that. I had to learn the hard way.

On the other hand, being a stubborn, learn-it-the-hard-way type has had its advantages, too: I'm able to empathize with other people who do things that way, too!

Now, one of the major keys to success in this business is *duplication*. Your sponsor helps you duplicate his or her efforts. You do the same thing with the people you sponsor, and so on down-the-downline.

So, if somebody along the line is the stubborn, "I'm going to do it my way" kind of person—like I was—what should you do with them?

Here's what Robert Natiuk did with me: He just stuck with me.

He never gave up on me—no matter how headstrong and street-stupid I acted. I asked him once why he did that, and here's what he said:

"Robert, never pre-judge people in this business. And never give up on people who are willing to learn. When you didn't take my advice seriously, I just pulled back a little. I let you go your own way, because I knew you were sincere and really wanted to be a success. But I never gave up on you—and what's more important, you never gave up on yourself. I knew you were a bright guy, and I knew you'd figure it out after you tried enough short cuts that didn't work."

Wise men and women make the best mentors. Patient ones, too. Natiuk's both wise and patient.

Be True To Yourself

More things I learned from Robert Natiuk:

"Robert, don't try to be somebody you're not. Speak from the heart and be yourself. Let the real you come out, let the inner marketing emerge from within you."

"Inner marketing"?

That's a term Robert invented to describe the real marketing power of this business—and it's the real key to success, as well. I can't do justice to the concept, so you should read his book, *The Power of Inner Marketing*, to reach a full understanding of it. The best thing I can do is to quote Shakespeare's great line:

"This above all: to thine own self be true."

That's close to what Natiuk means.

Natiuk also taught me the Value-for-Value principle.

A Business Based On Value

The bottom line of any Networking opportunity has got to come down to *Value for Value.*

Ultimately, the driving force behind any Network Marketing business is the product or service that you're offering. If the product doesn't offer the consumer real and tangible benefits, or if they can get the same results better or cheaper somewhere else—*forget it.*

There's another part of "value" that Natiuk taught me—*your own value.* "You need to be grateful for what you have," he told me, "while you're striving for what you want to be." It's the attitude-of-gratitude principle.

You see, quite often people in our business are not as happy as they should and could be. They're too busy comparing themselves to other people, looking in somebody else's wallet, striving in a "Life-will-be-perfect-when-I-have-[*blank*] . . ." sort of way. That's living in the future; and it's a future that may never arrive—until they change that "some day" orientation.

Natiuk taught me to honor the values, the important things that I have in my life right now, to be grateful for all I've accomplished, even while I was striving for more.

"After all," he would say, "thankfulness attracts many kinds of wealth to you. Be at peace with what you have now and who you are. Go on from there."

So true.

Then he asked:

"Robert, how high should a tree grow?"

I answered that one: "Depends on the kind of tree—and its environment."

"Good answer, Robert," he replied. "So how will you grow to your full potential?"

Right—by being myself (the kind of tree I am)—and consciously improving my environment.

One more Natiuk gem:

Q: How do you create loyalty?

A: By being integrated with life's highest values, and thus contributing to the good of others.

Remember those two, and you'll be a leader in this business for sure!

Don Failla—The Man with THE Question

Another of my mentors is Don Failla.

Don is one of the original masters of MLM. He's also a master at holding a carrot in front of people and having them respond positively to what he has to offer. Jim Rohn—another great teacher—says, "If people believe the promise, they'll pay the price." Failla is probably the best I've seen at positioning the "why's" of what we're doing in Network Marketing in just such a way that people will buy into them and *believe* the promise.

Don doesn't ask people if they want to "do the business." He asks them:

"Do you want to own your own life?"

That's a very different question—and a very powerful

one. Once they buy that concept, they're "lifers" in this business!

The second thing Failla taught me is to "let tools do the work."

What happens when you put the right tools—the letters, audio tapes, books, videos, brochures—properly in front of someone? They (the tools) ask and answer the right questions, each and every time. They do the explaining for you in such a way that when you meet face-to-face (or phone-to-phone), you can concentrate your own time and energy on the all-important personal part of your business relationship—which, of course, is the thing that the tools *can't* do.

We'll talk lots more about tools later on. For now, just know how very powerful they are in helping you build your business most effectively.

The Fun Of This Business Is—
This Business Is Fun!

Don and his wife Nancy also taught me that in this business, we need to *live* what we're selling, which is *fun*. They discovered that there's a direct relationship between the amount of fun you're having in Network Marketing and your ability to attract people *to* you and to doing the business *with* you.

When people perceive that we're "efforting"—that is, working real hard in doing the business—why would they want to join us? They already have a job where they work hard like that.

So Don sets an example by going out and living a life of fun.

He usually dresses in a Hawaiian shirt to show people that you don't need that tied-down professional look to be a successful business person—especially in Network Marketing.

Gold Ships

I also learned from Don that you want to focus your energies on the people who are producing the results in the business. You only want to work with the people who really have a sincere desire and are serious about doing the business.

In his book, *The Basics: How To Build A Large Successful Multi-Level Marketing Organization,* which is the best-selling Network Marketing book of all time, Don calls these people "the gold ships."

Now, what he's saying is that if you put a lot of energy into a person that doesn't have the desire, you're wasting both your time *and* theirs.

How do you know when people have the desire?

They let you know by their actions, or lack of actions. (We'll say more about this later.)

You Are Your Upline

Here's one more brilliant thing (among many) I learned from Don:

Once you sign up a brand new person, have that new person send records of their new applicants to their upline sponsors.

Then, have those upline people in turn send the new people a package welcoming them to the team. Have them include some valuable information in those packets, so the new people realize that there's more than just their own direct sponsor involved in their business opportunity helping them gain the lifestyle they want.

I tried it out; it works. In fact, it's brilliant—and powerful!

How Often Do You Speak With Your Mentors?

I speak with Natiuk, Failla and a couple other of my mentors often, even daily. I speak with others at least once a week.

I'll tell you something I've noticed about people who are successful in this business: Every one of them has a whole bunch of mentors, teachers and coaches. In fact, the more successful they are, the more mentors they have.

Mentors are coaches—they teach you the basics and they keep you on track. They are excellent resources for new ideas and new approaches you wouldn't normally think of by yourself. Consultant, teacher, counselor, coach, leader, director—these and more are all qualities of being a mentor.

It's often said that in Network Marketing,

"You're in business for yourself, but not BY yourself."

Go find the right mentors, ask them tough questions, and start listening to what they have to say.

I can say with confidence that I was not successful in this business until I had a few mentors and started staying in touch with them constantly. I also noticed that the more successful I became, the more mentors I had!

Then I noticed something else—the most important fact of all when it comes to mentors:

Mentors come first—THEN comes success!

So a real good Street Smart thing to do, right from the start of your Networking business career, is to get some mentors. Get the best ones you can find. And the more of them you get, the more successful you're likely to become.

One more piece of mentor wisdom:

"When the student is ready—the teacher will appear."

So be smart—and get ready right away!

Your Law Of Averages Improves With Time

Another of my mentors is a man I mentioned earlier, Jim Rohn. He wrote a book, *Seven Strategies to Success*, and a tape series, *Take Charge of Your Life*. *Take Charge . . .* is one of the most powerful tapes I've ever listened to— it's got some real gold nuggets of wisdom about life and work. One of those nuggets is about the law of averages.

No matter who you are, or what your prior experience, when you start to go out looking for people to join you in your new Networking business, you're going to get, oh, perhaps one out of ten people to join at first.

But as you keep talking with people, your learning curve continually improves. And with it, *your* law of averages improves, too. Not *the* law of averages, *your* law of averages.

Pretty soon, you're getting *three* out of ten . . . then four, five, and so on. *Everyone* goes through a learning curve and a law-of-averages curve. As you continually improve and practice whatever you're doing, that learning curve keeps getting better and better. It's one of those laws that just goes to show you: The world really is on your side!

Here's a quote of Jim's I love:

"If you do this business right, you can make a fortune and take a lot of good people with you."

That's the true essence of Network Marketing.

Rohn also taught me that you can't just sit there and wait for someone to come by and motivate you—or your people, for that matter. I mean, what if "someone" doesn't show up? Then where are you?

To be a success in Network Marketing, you've got to *motivate yourself!*

You Get What You Expect

Another mentor of mine is Dr. Robert Anthony, who talks about the "stream of life." Dr. Anthony says that you can get whatever you want from that stream of life depending upon *what you expect* from it.

Now, some people go down to the bank of the stream with a thimble in their hand, and guess what? They come back with a thimbleful of water.

Some go with a teaspoon—and they bring back, you guessed it, a teaspoonful of water.

You can only bring back as much as you're prepared to get. And guess what'll happen if you take a *bucket* with you? You'll come back with a bucketful!

What you bring with you to the stream of life is *your expectations*.

It's rare that someone who doesn't expect to get a whole lot from life gets any more than that. Sometimes, you'll meet people who are surprised by their success. But if you look closely, you'll find that they were really opening up more and more to the possibility of that success, even though they might not have been aware of it.

It's a law of human nature—you can't get more than you expect.

So, in the stream of Network Marketing, I suggest you walk around with a *truck* to put your success in. As for me, since I learned this principle, I've been driving a super-tanker!

Mail Bonding

Stephen Kenyon and Charles Possick have both taught me about how to create a prospecting and recruiting system around direct mail.

Now, there are people who look down on direct mail approaches to Network Marketing. I think that's crazy. Unless your entire business is done through local meetings,

Ermgard's latest umbrella opportunity mailing included sending 437 packets with complete product, compensation plans, testimonials and cover letters along with personalized, pre-registered distributor applications for all 26 of her 26 MLM companies. She called it "Trolling For Distributors."

chances are you're going to use lots of mail. So, it's best to learn from the masters how to do it successfully. That's what I did. As Wayne Dyer teaches: Don't limit the ways you have of attracting people—and using the mail is one very powerful way.

Possick has a lot of simple techniques that have a big impact.

One is to send out packets by "First Class Presort," which you can do through a mailing service or independent "post office box store" that will also mail and Fed-Ex letters. I send out "Welcome Paks" to all my new distributors by First Class Presort, and gain a significant savings over regular First Class. I just wait a little till I have a bunch (since you need a minimum of at least 100 for Presort), and then mail them all together. That idea alone has saved me hundreds of dollars on postage.

Here's another great thing Charles does: When he goes on a cruise or stays at a resort for a meeting, he gets postcards from the steamship line or hotel. (They give them away for free.) Then, he writes a handwritten note that fits on the card—something like, "Hi, what a great convention. We really missed you. Look forward to seeing you next year. Charles"—then takes it to his printer, has a couple hundred to a couple thousand printed up and mails them to all his people.

By networking with Kenyon for many years, I've been able to learn and benefit from his systematic approach to Networking by mail. This is a business of communication, regardless of what techniques are used to build the business. On a local basis, you can host sizzle sessions and various get-togethers to keep people informed and excited. When building long-distance with remote marketing techniques, you still need to communicate with your people to maximize productivity and minimize drop-outs. Stephen does this through a series of follow up letters, occasional cassette tapes, and newsletters.

Another neat communication idea we do together is to team up with several upline associates and a few key leaders in our downline, and everyone sends different welcome packages to the people just joining, as well as letters of introduction with relevant enclosures to key prospects. This team effort overwhelms people with follow up (overwhelms them in a good way, that is!) and really makes a big difference.

Stephen also taught me the importance of standing out in the mails. Your materials must be strikingly different to be effective, your mail-order materials must stand out head and shoulders above all the tacky, faded out, third generation photocopies that typically circulate within Network Marketing's "inner circle." Differentiate your materials and your approach like Stephen does, and your mail order presentation will command the attention it deserves.

Another effective idea I learned from the direct mail people is to include an opportunity note in every bill you pay. Can you imagine when was the last time that the person who sits there opening envelopes got a personal note from a bill-payer? Probably never! Sooner or later, one of these folks will give you a call!

Owning Your Life— Or Just Owning Your Own *Job?*

Another mentor of mine is Michael Gerber, author of the book, *The E Myth.*

This is the single best book on the business of business I've ever read. In *The E Myth,* Gerber talks about how to create a "turn-key operation," building a business as if you were going to franchise it hundreds of times. And that, of course, is just what we do in Network Marketing.

Gerber states that most small business people don't own their own businesses—they own their own jobs! In other words, they're still tied down to their "work" with chains ... it's just that now they're the ones who own the key. Is that ever true—even in Network Marketing.

Gerber had me pegged, right on the money. For a long time, I didn't see that the way I had it set up, my Networking business wasn't really freedom—it was just a job, even if it was one that I owned. I was just too close to it to see. Gerber helped me see that. And once I did, I went to work ON my business, instead of IN my business, and that's made all the difference in the world!

Here's what Gerber says to do:

Visualize your business as it will be when you've completed the process of building it. See the business as an accomplished fact—and then *go to work on that vision!*

Integrity and Partnership

Two more mentors of mine are Doris Wood, president of our industry trade association, the Multi-Level Marketing International Association (MLMIA), and John Milton Fogg, Editor of *Upline*™—"The Journal For Network Marketing Leaders."

I've learned a lot of things from Doris, but number one is that integrity is the absolute key to all that you do in this business. You've got to hold your integrity up to the light and scrutinize it—make sure that it's solid, and that it's what you're all about.

Doris also taught me to *first* check out the people who are behind the scenes running any Network Marketing company. That has turned out to be excellent advice—you can *usually* predict people's futures by their past.

John Fogg is one of that finest kind of mentors who is also a great friend. John contributes something to me every time we talk—which is at least once a week, and often more.

This guy's insights are matched only by his commitment to this industry. Both are extraordinary. His publication, *Upline*™, is the best. I give one as a gift to each person that I sponsor into the business. That way, I know *they* know the important why's and how's of our business.

What John has contributed to me most is *partnership*. Network Marketing is all about partnership, and John is a master at it. He's taught me how to create dynamic partnerships in my Network that have empowered everybody up and down the line.

Pearls of Wisdom

Four more important mentors: Tom "Big Al" Schreiter, John Kalench, founder and president of Millionaires In Motion, and two men, Jack Trout and Al Ries, who authored a book called *Positioning: The Battle for Your Mind.*

Tom Schreiter, a.k.a. "Big Al," has taught me so much, it's tough to put my finger on one or two things to single out, but I will. One of the most important things I've learned from Big Al is the necessity of building *loyalty* in your Network Marketing organization.

Here's how Big Al says you do this:

Find one person who's really hot on the business—and then *move in with them for six months!* After you do this four or five times, you've got a super-solid foundation for building a very successful business.

Why? Because when you've done this, your person now knows everything you know *plus* everything he or she already knew. Bingo! You don't need more than a handful of people like that in business with you to be a smashing success.

Which brings up an important point. This is a principle that often surprises people when they first hear it, but when you look at it carefully, it makes complete sense:

The most successful sponsors I know of in Network Marketing can point to TWO, THREE or FOUR leaders in their organizations who are responsible for generating most of their income.

These "key people" are loyal to you, because you've helped them become successful. And when they build the same kind of loyalty with *their* people, you've got one devoted and powerful Network! There's no fear about losing people to another opportunity. Makes good sense.

So, how do you find these "hot" people? According to Tom Schreiter, they're out there for the taking—they're like pearls. The biggest mistake people make, says Tom, is to open up an oyster, find it doesn't contain a pearl, and then try to do things to make it produce a pearl. You can see how silly that is, but people try to do it anyway.

Big Al says—jes' keep shuckin' dem oysters. Either there *is* a pearl inside—or there *isn't*. Your job is simply to find out which it's going to be, and move on.

I also love Big Al's simple one-two prospecting approach. He asks, "Do you know anybody who wants to earn extra income?" If the person says, "Yes," and it's *that person* who wants it, Big Al then asks, "Have you got seven to ten hours a week?" If the person says "Yes" again, that's it. It's time for them to take a closer look at your business opportunity.

It doesn't get any more straightforward—or easier— than that!

John Kalench wrote a terrific book entitled *The Greatest Opportunity in the History of the World.* After I read it, I said to myself, "Yeah! That's exactly what Network Marketing is!" And ever since I read John's book, I've looked at the business of talking to people about Network Marketing as if I were offering them a fabulous gift.

Which, in fact, I am—and so are you!

It's a whole different place to come from when you're prospecting.

John also wrote a book called *Being The Best You Can Be In MLM.* What I learned in that book was that you've got to be clear about the "Whys" of doing this business *before* you can succeed. To be successful, a person must be in touch with the reason they're doing the business.

In tough times—and *everyone's* got (or will have) those!—you need that clear "Why" to fall back on. It's a powerful anchor. Without it, it's pretty easy for a strong wind to set you adrift. In good times, you'll find those "Whys" are what pulls you forward to even greater achievements.

Jack Trout and Al Ries are two successful Madison Avenue marketers who wrote a book called *Positioning: The Battle For Your Mind.*

"Positioning" is the image people form in their minds about who you are, about what your product is, and about what value you and your products hold for them, relative to the competition.

One tremendously valuable thing I learned from it is that you only get one chance to make a first impression. That explains why it is that *how you present yourself*, your products and your Network Marketing opportunity is so very, very important.

The concept of "Positioning," and how it applies to what a Street Smart Networker does, is *so important* that we'll cover it some more later on.

There are many, many other mentors I've had, still have today and will have tomorrow.

Mentors are the richest possible source for ideas, problem-solving resources, touch-stones through tough times, and the very best way of all to keep you in action and productive in this business. Tell a mentor you're going to do something, and he or she will hold you to it. That one thing alone makes having them very worthwhile, indeed!

One last mentor I want to mention: Stephen Covey.

The Business of Shifting Paradigms

In his book, *The Seven Habits of Highly Effective People*, Covey tells an incredibly moving story to illustrate what a *"paradigm shift"* is.

A "paradigm" is the particular way we see things. We each have our own paradigm of how we think the world works. Sometimes, our paradigms overlap with those of other people. Sometimes, an entire culture shares a given paradigm.

For example, people in America share a paradigm of sales and selling. There's a prevailing paradigm about politics and politicians . . . about the state of the economy . . . about the value of meat-eating versus vegetarianism . . . and so forth. Paradigms aren't set in concrete—and they're not necessarily based on the absolute truth of the facts. Paradigms are simply currents of opinion—and they tend to shape the way we see everything.

One of the things you'll be doing as a street smart Networker is changing people's paradigms: About Network Marketing, about employment and opportunity, about sales and selling, and even about themselves and their own potential.

In a sense, supporting people's constructive paradigm shifts is our principle "job description."

Covey tells a story about a personal paradigm shift:

One day, he's riding the New York City subway. It's a quiet morning, so he's really put off when some guy comes in with two very loud and obnoxious children. These kids are tearing around the subway car, stepping on people, screaming . . . they even take some guy's newspaper and throw it all over the place. And the whole time these kids are going nuts, their father just sits there, doing nothing.

Finally, Covey can't contain himself any longer, and he leans over and says something like, "Hey, your kids are going crazy here. Why don't you control them?"

And the guy looks up at him with this far-off expression and says:

> *"Oh. You're right. I'm sorry. We just came from the hospital where their mother died. I guess they don't know how to handle that. I don't either. I'm sorry they're disturbing you. I'll stop them now."*

Whamm!!!

Talk about a paradigm shift!

What I learned from that story is also taught in the old Native American wisdom that says:

> *"Before you pass judgment on somebody, walk a mile in his moccasins."*

Thanks to Dr. Covey, I am a lot more careful about

judging people.

To judge or not to judge—that's a critical point in this business.

I've sponsored people into Network Marketing who I thought were going to go all out and really become successful with it, people I thought would make themselves and me a fortune—only to have them drop out in four weeks.

I've sponsored others who, I was sure, didn't stand a chance—then watched them become super-stars.

You never know—so don't even guess. And remember what Robert Natiuk said about sticking with people and not giving up on them. Be like a postage stamp—stick to them till they get where they're going!

The results we're getting right now are the net accumulation of our belief systems—paradigms—and how we see things. Our attitudes toward reality create how we see things—which in turn creates the reality itself. Key point. Change your beliefs and you change the world. That's when quantum leaps begin to happen throughout your life!

Covey also created a tape from a book he wrote, *Principle-Centered Leadership*. It's the final piece of mentorship I want to tell you about here.

In the tape, Covey asks his listeners to imagine when they were back in college, did they ever see anybody who crammed their way through school? If you didn't, I can tell you what it's like. I used Cliff Notes, bought notes for courses I didn't want to show up for, crammed for exams ... the whole crazy routine.

Then Covey asks, Could you do that on a farm?

Can you imagine cramming on a farm?! What a great image! No way. If you don't get the animals fed, if you don't plant and harvest at the right time, there's no way you can fake it through.

Covey points out that in college, you can get a *degree* taking all the short cuts, but what you can't get is an *education.*

It's the same in Network Marketing.

Sure, you can zip through, cramming and taking short cuts, but in the end, all you'll do is look good to some people. Your check won't reflect anything but the truth of what you're up to. Some people can shuck-'n'-jive for a good time in this business, but it always—*always*—catches up with them.

Like my mentor Robert Natiuk said to me:

"There are no short cuts on the road to success."

There Are No "Good Directions" For A Sunday Drive

Why not? Because road directions are useless when you're not really going anywhere.

If you don't know what you want, then you're just out for *a Sunday drive.*

A Sunday drive is when you pack up the kids in the car, and you and your spouse just take off down the road. When you come to an intersection, you don't have to be concerned which way you turn. Doesn't matter. You're out for a Sunday drive. You don't have a destination—"getting somewhere" isn't the point.

The point of a Sunday drive is just to *go* somewhere—*anywhere.* It doesn't really matter what direction you go—as long as you end up back at home in your driveway, eventually.

Now, imagine doing your Networking business like a Sunday drive . . .

Do you know people in this business who are doing it that way?

What do you think are their chances for success?

To succeed in Network Marketing—or in anything else, for that matter—you've got to know where you're going.

Sure, the trip itself is where the fun is, but a trip that simply goes in circles is no fun—unless you really *are* literally out for a Sunday drive! And the aimlessness of a Sunday drive is death (or at least, major paralysis!) in this business. When you know where you want to end up— and you've got a map or some idea of your overall direction—then when you come to an intersection, you can say, "Turn left," or "Turn right."

It's called getting there *on purpose.*

Otherwise, the only way you'll get someplace you like getting to will be by luck.

"What's the matter, Robert, don't you believe in luck?"

Sure, luck is important. But do you want to trust your life, your future and the welfare of your family and *their* future—to luck? No way.

So, how do you know where you want to go?

Two things: *goals* and *beliefs.*

Your goals are your destination, where you want to be. Without them, life's a Sunday drive for you.

Your beliefs are your "habitudes," as my friend John Fogg calls them. Habitudes, says John, are simply *habits of attitude*, which either assist you to accomplish your goals, or act as obstacles to prevent you from accomplishing your goals.

Either way, they exist in your mind simply as habits you have developed, just like you've developed habits of posture or speech. And the good news is, habits can be changed—and you can change them to help you accomplish what you need and want.

And that's what we'll talk about next.

Chapter Three
Where It's Really At

YOUR HABITUDES ARE THE UNDERLYING FOUNDATION that governs all your actions. They're the cornerstone, the root of your perception of reality. Like one of Stephen Covey's *paradigms*. And if you don't think something is real or possible for you, you won't do it—even if you say or think you want to.

If you've got a belief that you *cannot* earn $10,000 a month (or put another way, if you *do not* have the belief that *you can* earn $10,000 a month), then there's no way you'll ever earn that kind of income.

None.

In a recent issue of *Upline*™, Rocklin Duffy wrote:

"Without belief, there is no action. Information does not create action. Belief creates action—it's a fuel for action. Greater belief—more intense fuel for action, more power."

And being in powerful action is a big key to success in this or any other business.

Your mind—all of our minds—are very much like computers. What's the first law of computing?

GIGO. "Garbage In—Garbage Out."

You put bad stuff into your computer—and bad stuff will come out. Usually, even *more bad* than what you put in!

The mind's the same way—GIGO. And the truth is, if you're like most people, you've been putting in a ton of "garbage" and "bad stuff" ever since you were a little kid, and probably never even realized it.

"No, No, No, No, No, No . . ."

Did you know that little kids hear the word "No" *17 times* for every "Yes" they hear?! Incredible! And this isn't just my opinion, it's backed up by scientific studies.

Think about what that means to those little kid minds— little minds, don't forget, that are building strong habitudes twelve ways.

Now, get out your calculator: Let's say Little Kid X hears 22 "Yes's" in one day. How many "No's" is Little Kid X going to hear? Hmm . . . that's –

374 of them!

Now, that's a lot of negativity for such an open, impressionable young mind. 136,500-plus "No's" in one year. By the time Little Kid X is eight or nine years old, he or she has gotten tons of "No" input—close to a million negatives.

And remember, we call these "the formative years."

It's no wonder that as adults, most of us have "can't-do" beliefs. We've been programmed that way for years and years—literally a million times or more.

GIGO.

So, what do we do about it?

Reprogramming. And what that takes is just changing two small things—actually, changing *one* thing, two times.

The "G" in GIGO stands for "Garbage," right? Well, we're going to change that "G" so that it stands for "Gold" instead.

Gold In—Gold Out.

A whole new GIGO—one that works *for* you.

Your Habitudes

Now, it takes a conscious effort to make this happen. The key is those habitudes.

Your beliefs—what you expect from yourself and from your world—have become habits for you. Habits are something you don't think about anymore. They're things you do, or think, or believe—automatically.

You don't think about tying your shoe laces—you just do it. You have habits of thought just like that, too. They're your habitudes—attitudes you have that have become habitual. You don't think about them anymore. You just have them. And as you've seen from the scientific research, the majority of habitudes you and I have are "No" habits—what we *can't* do, *can't* have, and *can't* become.

We got these habitudes over time, slowly, one by one. So, that's how we change them—one by one. The good news is, we don't have to take as long to change them as we did making them. Why? Because this time, we're doing it *on purpose.*

It's About Changing Your Mind

Don't bother trying to get rid of bad habitudes! If you do that, you'll just leave an empty space which your mind will feel compelled to rush in and fill up—like a vacuum. And it doesn't matter how much will power you think you've got; in fact, having more will power just fills up the spaces faster and harder!

What you want to do is to *replace* those old, negative habitudes with positive, supportive habitudes—just like we replaced the "G-stands-for-Garbage" in GIGO with a new "G-stands-for-Gold."

What you want to do is to *change your mind.*

Have you ever changed your mind before? How hard was that?

Not very, I'll bet. We all change our minds all the time.

It's easy.

So now, what you're going to do is change your mind systematically, on purpose, when *you* want to.

Pick a habitude—any habitude.

I'll use one of mine as an example: Playing basketball.

I play basketball for exercise and fun. I was in my twenties when I started playing and I learned the game pretty quickly. I've got strong hands and I enjoy competitive sports, because I'm a competitive kind of guy. I'm also good at team sports, because I'm a real team player.

But I've got the wrong build.

You see, most basketball players are thin, wiry types. I'm not. I'm not all that tall—and I'm not all that thin, either! All in all, I'm definitely *not* your typical basketball body. Besides, I never played the game in high school or college.

But I love basketball!

Now, I developed as a defensive player rapidly. I could mess up other people's plays and get in their way with the best of them—but I had no confidence in my ability to shoot. I'd steal the ball away from the other team, break down court, have a clear shot at the basket, but instead of taking the open shot myself, I'd pass it off to a teammate.

I had it wired up in my brain that I was good at defense—and I was. I also had it wired up that I wasn't a shooter—and I wasn't. The fact that I was such a good team player actually gave me an excuse to avoid shooting. I'd just pass to a guy who could make the shot and prove that I'd made the right choice by not shooting myself.

Other people would talk to me about my game—you know, criticize how I played, what I was doing wrong, where I needed to improve. Lots of that was good and valuable stuff, but the remarks about my offensive play didn't help me at all. They all went into this internal hopper that I'd labeled, "Robert's Not A Shooter."

Then I came across a study that was done a number of

years ago in a college with the intramural basketball teams. It went like this:

They split the kids into three groups. The first spent one half hour every day shooting foul shots in the gym. The second group spent one half hour imagining they were shooting *and sinking* foul shots—but these kids weren't in the gym. They were sitting on chairs in a room somewhere. The third group didn't do anything.

The researchers had tested the kids before the experiment began, so they knew how well they could shoot when they started out. What happened after one month of this research setup is truly amazing:

The group that didn't do anything showed zero improvement. In fact, they'd lost a couple of points. The first group, the kids who'd practiced in the gym, had improved 24 percent. And the group that had practiced *in their minds,* improved 23 percent—only *one percent less* than the guys who worked out every day "for real"!

After I read that, I started taking and sinking shots on the "court" in my mind. And guess what? I also started sinking them in the games right away. I pretty quickly built up my confidence to a point where I'd take that shot which before I would have given away. And from that point on, when I'd hear people criticize me for missing an easy one, it no longer mattered to me at all. I took their comments as simply not personal. I would distance that and affirm that it was not like me to miss a shot. What *was* personal was my being a successful shooter. That's the only thing I let affect me—and I put that thought on center stage in my mind, and it magnified.

Today, I play basketball with guys who played in college and I more than hold my own. I'm known as a tough competitor, a formidable defender and—if I do say so myself—a darn good shot maker. It's a habit with me.

Positive self-talk and creative visualization is truly powerful stuff. And it works.

Now, I don't pretend to know exactly *how* it works. I've

heard all kinds of ideas about how we bring up pictures in our minds . . . and about the subconscious mind . . . how every image we have like this the mind accepts as real and true . . . But however it works, the bottom line is, with effort, we can reprogram all our habitudes into ones that support us.

And here's another piece of good news about habitudes:

You don't need to know which negative habitudes you have in place in order to change them.

Instead, just pick a bunch of positive ones that serve you—and do *them*. The replacement process happens automatically.

No matter in what area of your life you want to form good habitudes, you can do it using the same, simple techniques. Just make up a positive statement. Make it past tense—as an accomplished fact. Use your name, first, last or both.

You can jazz the process up (make it faster and more powerful) if you simply pause a moment whenever you see one of these positive habitude signs of yours, close your eyes (don't do this while driving, please!) and imagine yourself, *being* whatever it is, in full detail—sights, smells, sounds, everything.

For example, I imagined myself being the star player on a team that wins a major basketball game. People were cheering. I got this big trophy—*and* a check for one million dollars! Boy, did I feel fantastic! (*"One million dollars?!"* Hey, it's my imagination. I'll set it up any way I want!)

You get the idea. Make it a really full and rich experience. And don't forget, your mind is hearing all this and seeing all this and saying to itself,

"Hey, look at that, Robert's team won the basketball game AGAIN. That's the 32nd game this season! Gee . . . he's getting really good at this!"

This is so powerful, yet so simple. You've just got to try it.

Make a list—do it right now, while it's fresh in your mind—of three or four new habitudes that you'd really love to have. Write them down in the spaces below. Remember to use your name and make them as if they were true for you, *right now.*

" _____ (Your name) is a millionaire ... is a very successful networker ... is slim, trim and beautiful ..." Whatever works for you—whatever you want. Write down four of them now:

1. *Penny lives in a beautiful new house that meets all her needs.*

2. *Penny is a multi-millionaire over and over.*

3. *Penny is slender, beautiful and healthy.*

4. *Penny is happy beyond her wildest dreams.*

Great. Now, get some 3 x 5 cards or Post-it Notes™ and paste a bunch of them up all around the house, next to your phone, in your car. Read them every day, as often as you can.

Put Your Mouth Where Your Money Will Be

Here's a piece of doable magic that will accelerate all your habitude-changing work *big time!* It's called a "self-talk tape."

Once you've got a fistful of positive habitudes down on paper, I want you to arrange them into a script that takes anywhere from 30 seconds to one or two minutes to read out loud. Here's what you're going to do next:

- Purchase a 30-, 60- or 90-second "endless loop" tape, the kind they make for answering machines.

- Set up your telephone answering machine to record your self-talk tape.

    And by the way, *don't* try this on a regular tape machine. If you do, the endless loop tape will just keep going and you'll re-record *over* what you just recorded. Answering machines stop automatically when the tape has completed one revolution.

    Save yourself all the headaches and record your tape on your answering machine. Just use the outgoing message tape side of the recorder to do your recording like you do with your greeting.

- Get a piece of Baroque music for the background—one of those slow *Adagio* types, like the famous Pachelbel Canon or Bach's "Air on the G String." This kind of music has been successfully tested to dramatically increase your openness to the message recorded over it, and your memory, too.

    Use a second tape player or record player to have your background music playing in the background as you record your self-talk tape.

- Repeat each habitude *three times:*
    The first time, say "I _____ ..." whatever your

39

habitude is.

The second time, use "He" or "She."

The third time, use your name. Here's an example of one of my habitudes and how it goes on the tape:

"I am slim and trim—the perfect picture of health and aliveness."

"He is slim and trim—the perfect picture of health and aliveness."

"Robert Butwin is slim and trim—the perfect picture of health and aliveness."

Here's what this does: it programs your mind in all the most powerful ways you can, all at the same time.

Three is the magic number. Scientists have found that we grasp things best in a pattern of repeating it three times.

Also, by having it be "I," "He" or "She," and "Your Name," you deliver the message in all the ways in which you normally get input: (1) from yourself, (2) from strangers, and (3) from people who know you. That's how you formed the habitudes you've got now, and that's the perfect way to make new ones.

Now, once you've got your tape, *play it everywhere, every chance you get!*—in the car, in the shower, while you're getting dressed, mowing the lawn, jogging, etc. The very best time to play it is last thing at night and first thing in the morning. That's when your mind is most receptive.

You can also set the volume very low and play it all night long, too. That way, even though you aren't aware of it, your positive message is still getting through. Your ears and your subconscious mind are wide awake, even when "you" are sound asleep.

And just think of this: In a very short time, you will have heard enough positive input to counter a lifetime of negativity! It's true. This is a super way to "re-program" all your habitudes for success.

Now, let's get specific about establishing habitudes that will empower you in the business of your Networking business. And by the way, it wouldn't be a bad idea to make a Networking self-talk tape as well. I can't imagine a more powerful way to create a super-positive set of success habitudes for building your Network Marketing business.

Five Powerful Habitudes for Network Marketing

I've made a list of five habitudes that will help you to be successful in Network Marketing.

Habitude #1: A Positive Belief In Network Marketing

As the title of one of John Kalench's books puts it, Network Marketing is *The Greatest Opportunity in the History of the World!*

Now, what do you think: If you had a habitude that had you believing *that*—what do you think would be your chances for success in this business?

High up in the 90 percentiles—and that's a fact! There's nothing you can do, or think, or say, that's as powerful as having an absolute, rock-solid, unshakable belief that this industry is the greatest opportunity ever!

Have you ever heard the old adage that, when you start something new, your success is 90 percent enthusiasm and 10 percent know-how? It's true. And many people who really know very little about how to do Network Marketing succeed in the beginning just because they believe so strongly in what a wonderful business this is.

Think about it this way: What you're offering people is not just a "business opportunity." What you're offering people is a lifeboat on the stormy seas of today's employment picture. No, make that "UNemployment picture"!

Remember "job security"? That concept has about as much relevance to today's workaday world as Ozzie and Harriet represent the typical urban family of the '90s. There IS NO job security anymore! That means that to create some insurance for your future and your kids' futures, you virtually HAVE to create some sort of income portfolio; you can't rely on a job that could be gone in a year, a month, or a week. And imagine how much easier and less stressful it is to create that portfolio NOW, with Network Marketing—rather than waiting till you're staring down the gun barrel of unemployment!

Now, picture this: Say you're on the deck of an ocean liner, in a storm, and you see someone out there in the water about to drown, and you're standing right next to a lifeboat—do you hesitate, wondering about the real value of this particular boat, and whether you'd be imposing on the person to suggest they get in . . . or do you lower the boat?!

That's exactly what you're up to here.

Another aspect of this first habitude is to have the belief that, if people really understood what Networking is about, *everybody* would want to be involved!

Now, if that's what you truly believe, how do you think you'll act with people? It's not hard to imagine: Someone who has a belief like that will offer people the opportunity to get involved in this business *as if it were a gift*. And it is!

That's the power of "Inner Marketing."

"I'm not prospecting or recruiting. I'm offering you a gift of incredible value—want to take a look at it?"

Powerful habitude!

Another thing that this kind of habit-of-attitude brings about is the genuine desire to educate and contribute to people.

You know that when people really understand what Network Marketing is, how it works and what it has to offer, *they want in!* So your approach begins to come from helping to educate them—helping them to understand what this business is *really* all about. And what do you think people's response to you will be?

Well, I can tell you from experience: it will be good. You're not trying to sell them anything. You're helping to educate them. That's a whole different ball game. That's catching bees with honey, because people really do love to learn—especially about things that will get them extra money to buy the freedom they've always wanted and to create a more meaningful life.

So, habitude *numero uno*—Network Marketing is the greatest opportunity in the history of the world!

Habitude #2: This Is A Great Company!

The second habitude is a strong belief in the company that you're representing. Can you imagine someone's chances for success if that person thinks the company he or she is with is "just okay"? No way!

Get in the habit of holding up your company as one of the leaders in our industry. See it as a company with integrity, having a mission for being in business, one with a passion for its distributors' welfare—and that of *their* customers, too. Hold its management in high esteem. Be a champion for your company.

Of course, it won't work to pretend this is true if you don't actually believe it is so. Make sure that you DO believe in the company that you represent—and then, with that as a foundation, practice keeping that belief up front, center stage, when you talk with others.

Now, all of this does not mean that you put other companies down. NEVER, EVER DO THAT!!! Here's the standard answer I recommend for questions about other companies:

"I don't know about such-and-such company. I'm with so-and-so company—let me tell you why it is my choice."

In Network Marketing, when you put other companies down, you put down all of Network Marketing itself. Just think about it: Why would anyone want to join your company if it were the *only one in the entire industry* that had good products, good people and a good plan? Great, you've got a good program (so *you* say)—within a crummy industry ... They'll head for the hills!

Stick to being a cheerleader for *your company*—not a detractor of others.

And what if you can't? What if the company you're with doesn't have its act together ... doesn't have integrity ... doesn't treat its people fairly?

Give them your best shot. Work with them. Help them to become better and better. If they don't—or won't ... GET OUT!

That's all there is to say about it.

You and your Network Marketing company are partners. If you don't love and respect your partner, you have no business being in business together.

You've got to have a strong abiding belief in your company.

Habitude #3: Believe In Your Product

Remember what Robert Natiuk taught me about "Value for Value"? Well, first and foremost, Value for Value refers to *the value of your products*.

Here is one of the most tried and true Network Marketing principles:

"You've got to be a product of the product."

That simply means, you've got to use the products yourself—aggressively, passionately. You've got to love

them, swear by them and think they're just great!
Now, I know some of you are thinking:

*"It's a business. Of course the product has to be good,
but . . . I mean . . . IBM people don't necessarily LOVE
their computers. I've seen employees from one store
shop at a competitor's place. What's the big deal?"*

The big deal is, this is Network Marketing. What drives
this business is word of mouth, the most powerful form of
marketing in the world. If you don't love your products, you
can't expect anyone else to care about them. And in this
business, if you don't have *that*—you don't have *anything*.

Great, unique, special products that are in high demand,
are the Network Marketer's stock in trade. Without such
a stellar product or service, you've got an uphill battle to
wage. (And without at least a product or service of some
value, even if it's not stellar, then you're not in Network
Marketing: You're operating a chain letter or pyramid
scheme—*and that's illegal!)*

You've got to have a product or service that knocks
people's socks off. That's how you build the retail side of
your business. Remember, this isn't "sales" in the traditional sense—so you can't run around with a product that
needs to be *sold*. You've got to have a product that's SO
good, that you like SO much, that all you need to do is
simply tell people how great it is and what it's done for
you, and then ask them if they want to try it—with a
money-back guarantee if they're not thrilled.

That scenario is why Network Marketing is so powerful.
It's hard to resist such a win-win proposition:

*"Fantastic product, I love it, you will, too—and if you're
in any way disappointed, you'll get all your money back."*

Bingo!
And here's another reason why you've got to be a product

of your product: More successful distributors come from the ranks of satisfied customers than from anywhere else. So you'd better have a product line that you can champion!

And another: You can have a network of a thousand people, but if no one orders and uses the products—you've got *no business,* and you get *no check!*

You want to have products that are *SO* good ... that represent *SUCH GREAT* value ... that people would flock to buy them even if there were no money-making opportunity involved at all.

Here is a real acid test for any Network Marketing opportunity:

If the company were to go out of business tomorrow, would you liquidate your inventory immediately, or would you call the company to find out if there were any way you could obtain more of the product?

Believe in your products big time! It's a key to Network Marketing success.

Habitude #4: "I Will Succeed!"
Do you know what is the most common verb in the English language? The word "will."

"I am a great success—I WILL succeed!"
"I am a great success—I WILL succeed!"
"I am a great success—I WILL succeed!"
"I am a great success—I WILL succeed!"
"I am a great success—I WILL succeed!"
"I am a great success—I WILL succeed!"
"I am a great success—I WILL succeed!"

Quick now: Will you succeed—Yes or No?

Ask yourself, "What will it take to succeed?—Am I willing to do what it takes?" If your answer is not a resounding "Yes!" then the first obstacle that comes your way will likely be your reason to quit.

Let me put it to you this way: Say we're standing out beside a schoolyard sandbox, and I go over and put four of the biggest diamonds you've ever seen down in the sand. I mix the sand around, shoveling it all up, then I say:

"Okay, take this sifter and go dig up the diamonds."

So, you take a big shovelful, sift it, and—shoot, no diamonds. Too bad. Oh, well, nothing to do now but quit, right? You've tried one shovelful, might as well walk away now, before you get your arms too tired, right?

No way! Hey, you *saw* me put the diamonds in there. You *know* they're there. You'll shovel that whole box empty before you quit, and you won't be content to stop until you have all four of the diamonds you saw me put into the sandbox!

Well, I wish I could give you a God's-eye view of the world and all the people in it to prove to you that there *ARE* four diamonds in the sandbox of life just waiting to come into business with you.

I promise you, they're out there. And you'll find them— if you just don't quit sifting the sand.

"But I have absolutely no idea of how to do it . . ."

That doesn't matter—*whatsoever*! It only matters that you believe you *will*—and persist to take some action. With that powerful, positive attitude, formed into a mental habit, you'll *find* the "How."

Often people are stopped when they don't know how to do something. That's too bad.

If you've watched any of the James Bond films, you know that secret agent 007 was *always* getting himself into jams. He'd walk right up to the enemy's stronghold and sit there having a drink with his foe Dr. No. He'd have no idea of *how* to defeat his enemy—just a rock solid belief in the fact that he *would* win. That's the kind of habitude you've got to get into your mind about your success in Network Marketing.

One way to empower this belief is to be very clear about WHY you're in this business. The bigger your *why*, the better.

Let's say you're in Network Marketing because you want to earn a few hundred dollars a month. That's one "Why."

Now, let's say your goal is to earn a million dollars a year to pay for a series of schools for underprivileged kids.

Which one of those two "Why's" do you think will get you out of bed in the morning—like a rocket to the top?

Having a monster *why* generates all kinds of power for accomplishment. It also tends to enroll a lot of powerful people in helping you accomplish your dreams. That's a real key to success in this business—or in any other. It's what Mark Yarnell calls, "Having a goal bigger than you are." Mark says it's one of the central keys to massive success in this business. He's right.

Now, don't forget *yourself* here. Truth is, until you take care of yourself, you can't provide for others. I'm not suggesting a "me first" habitude—just "me, too."

So, get to work on creating the habitude of "I *will* succeed!"

Habitude #5: A Master of Show and Tell

"Network Marketing is a teaching business." So say Don and Nancy Failla—and just about everybody else who really knows what our business is about.

Get to work right away on establishing a habitude that you are a Master of Show and Tell . . . you are a Master Teacher, an empowerment specialist.

More than in any other business in the world, your success in Network Marketing depends directly on your ability to help other people be successful. And by the way, don't be shy about teaching them to be even better than you are. Just think about what kind of success you'll have if you teach your people how to outdo you!

If you've got this ability already—to have your students surpass you—great! If you don't have it yet—*get it*. And the way to begin and sustain this all-important belief is to create and constantly recreate the habitude that *you are a master at teaching people to succeed.*

That's called, *being a Star-Maker.*

Those are the belief systems, the essential habitudes, that you need to have to be successful in this business.

I Believe . . . "You're Crazy!"

I know that a lot of this belief stuff strikes some people as crazy—at least at first. I mean, how can you sit there and say to yourself, "I believe I will succeed," if you've never done anything like this before—or worse, if you've tried before *and failed!*

Look, nobody had ever put anybody on the moon when President John F. Kennedy committed our entire country to the space program. Charles Lindbergh had never flown solo across the Atlantic ocean, and neither, for that matter, had anyone else! Thomas Edison never made a light bulb before, and he reportedly *failed* 999 times before he got one to work.

And there's an interesting one: Edison declared that he *NEVER* "failed"—he *succeeded 999 times* in learning how *not* to make a light bulb.

There's nothing wrong with failing, as long as you realize that you're always "failing towards success."

"Well," you may say, "that's fine for a famous inventor like Edison—but this is the real world. When you fail in business, it's over."

Perhaps so, in *conventional* business, but not Network Marketing. Think about it: In what other business can you fail, even over and over, and *not* get fired?

Compare that to what passes today for "job security"!

So, don't think for a moment you have to have proof-positive before you can create a successful habitude. Truth is, the further from the conditions of the moment it seems to you, the better. That way, when your mind does start to change and move in favor of your new belief, it will really pick up steam, moving you faster and faster toward your goals.

And goals are exactly what we need to talk about next.

CHAPTER FOUR

Going for the Gold

YOU'VE ALL HEARD OF "GOAL SETTING," RIGHT? GOOD. What I want to talk about with you here is *Gold Setting.* Because that's what it really is—*Going For the Gold.*

I am probably one of the best Gold-setters of all time! That's because I've set so many of them.

For example, 18 years ago, I used to smoke. I wanted to stop, so I did. And it felt so good to accomplish that, I did it again, and again ... In fact, I think I quit more than 100 times over a period of years.

Same thing with my weight loss "Golds." One time, I lost 65 pounds *in three months* and kept it off a couple of years—and then put it back on. I've been consistently setting Golds that I'm going to lose weight, about how much I'm going to earn, about all sorts of things I want and dream about.

Yes, I am definitely one of the best Gold-setters ever.

Only problem is, being good at Gold-setting is *nothing!*

Being good at Gold-*GETTING*, now, that really *is* something!

Step One: Believing You *Can*

In the previous chapter, we talked about your habitudes and beliefs. One thing that keeps Gold-setting from becoming Gold-*getting* is the critical question of whether or not you believe you can accomplish your Golds—any of them. All the good Golds, even the really Golden Golds, are no good, not worth a plugged nickel—if they come up against a habitude that you can't have them.

So, that's the place to start.

If you need to, go back a chapter and brush up on creating habitudes that will enable you to get and keep the Golds you set. A simple, "I am accomplishing all my Golds . . . I deserve to achieve all my Golds . . . _____ (your name) is a person who sets and gets (his or her) Golds every day!" You get the idea.

Remember, don't bother setting Golds you don't believe you deserve and can achieve. And if you don't have that belief, rather than backing off your Golds because you think they're too big, go hit up a new habitude that says you can have that big, bright Gold, too.

Make Your Golds Hard and Fast

Now, don't get uneasy. What I mean by *hard* and *fast*, doesn't have anything to do with working extra hard or struggling to reach your Golds—nor, how quick a time limit you have to achieve them. But it is about *time* in a way.

Do you remember the Biblical parable about a house built on sand? Well, it just isn't strong and doesn't last long. It has no bedrock to lay a foundation on. It's not *grounded* in reality.

Like houses, Golds need to be built on solid foundations, too. The way to do that is to make them specific and measurable, and to include a "by when" for each one.

"By when" means you'll accomplish or achieve the Gold by some specific date. That grounds your Gold for real. Do not establish any Gold that doesn't have a date *by when* you intend to accomplish it. No date—and it's not a real Gold. Without a "by when" date, we have the tendency to set the Gold back, and back, and back. No date, and our Gold always lives in the future—and it's a vague, unde-termined, never-gonna-get-there future, too! Remember:

There are no unrealistic goals—only unrealistic time frames.

What's more, you want to train your mind to perform *when you want.* A time-by-when is just a tool to help you achieve your Gold. That's all.

"Measurable" means that you have a clear, specific way to know when you've achieved it. A Gold that isn't mea-surable is a hope and a prayer, at best.

You should also be able to measure your Gold along the way. For example, you should be able to know when you're 20 percent there, half-way there, or 90 percent there. That way, you get to see yourself making undeniable, clear-cut progress—to *know* that you're lopping off another and then another chunk of your Gold.

And you know what that does? It gives you *momentum,* which is one thing it takes to reach and accomplish all your Golds. Seeing consistent and continual success begins to build and build on itself; it actually adds to your powers of accomplishment.

"Specific" refers to making your Golds *detailed.* "Get a car" is one thing. "Have a black Mercedes" (and yes, "by such and such a date") is quite another. The more specific, the clearer a picture it is—the more likely you'll believe it. Which, of course, is exactly what you need to do.

Now that I've said that, I want to add a twist on tra-ditional goal-setting:

Make your Golds specific—and leave some room for the unexpected.

Let me explain.

At one point, I had a Gold of earning a Mercedes (since then, I've actually earned two of them)—in fact, I had a Gold of earning "a Mercedes 560 SL in the color black." And as I'd learned through books and tapes on goal-setting, I visualized it, put pictures up on my refrigerator, the whole routine. Good, we're all set ...

Well, guess what? I ended up getting a Mercedes—but it wasn't a 560, and the color was gold, not black. And when I got it, was I upset that it wasn't a black SL? Are you kidding? Hey, I got the Mercedes!

You see, the specific model and color had helped me make the picture real and the Gold concrete, which helped me earn it—but those particular details, as it turned out, actually didn't matter to me at all.

You see, although it's essential that you make your Golds specific and measurable, there's a potential pitfall there, too:

Our pictures of what we want or expect aren't always accurate—and even when they are, they're going to change.

Here's what happens: You've got this Mercedes Gold, and some guy shows up with a Rolls Royce, and you say:

"Oh, thanks—but I've got this picture of a Mercedes on my fridge, so ... I guess you'll have to take the Rolls back. Thanks anyway."

Right? *Come on!*

Okay. That's a ridiculous example, but you get the point. Make your Golds specific—but don't get your mind stuck in the concrete. Leave room for changes and surprises.

And while you're leaving room for change, it's time to talk about going to ...

The Heart of the Matter

Your Golds will be far, *far* more powerful if, when you're making them, you go to *the heart of the matter.*

Our mental pictures of what *we think we want* are just that—mental pictures, thoughts. And thinking is *not* an exact science.

I think stuff all the time. Thoughts come and go with me. I'll bet they do with you, too.

So when you're creating a Gold, watch out for the coming and going of your thoughts. The way to do this is to focus your Gold setting on what's *behind* your thoughts. Here's what I mean by that.

Think of a Gold you have right now—and for this example, think of some*thing* you want, like a car, a house, a trip ... pick a thing, any thing.

Now, when you've pictured that, ask yourself: "What

will that provide for you?"

Now, when you have pictured *that*, ask this: "And what will *that* provide for you?"

Now, keep doing this *until you cannot think of anything further that having "that" would provide.* In other words, when you can't get any more answers to that question—when you've peeled away all the layers of your Gold. When that happens, you've hit bedrock—you're at *the heart of the matter.* You've got your hands on the *essence* of what you want.

I first learned this business of "essence" from John Kalench's book, *Being The Best You Can Be In MLM,* and it is an incredibly powerful principle!

What makes "essence" so powerful? When you know the essence of what you want, two things happen.

First, you can create that essence—whatever it is—as one of your habitudes.

For example, let's say you want a new car—a Lincoln, Lexus, Mercedes, etc. Okay: What will having that Mercedes provide for you?

"Well, it'll be a fantastic feeling knowing that I've got one of the best cars money can buy ... driving in real style."

Okay; so, imagine having those feelings right now—what do they provide for you?

"Confirmation, recognition, that I've made my success happen."

Now, if that's bedrock for you, if that's bottom line what having that Mercedes is going to provide you, then follow this:

What better way to bring that car into your driveway than to know that the essence of that car for you is "recognition of my success"—and then create

*a habitude, right now, of being constantly recognized
for your success!*

Here you are, empty driveway and all, running around
with a growing, glowing habitude of recognition and success. How long do you think it will be before that recognition of success shows up as a car in your driveway?

Put in place a powerful habitude that gives you the
essence of your Gold, and the Gold itself will appear one
day as if by magic. It's not really magic at all, just how
the mind works—but that's how it'll seem!

And here's the second thing knowing the "essence" of
your Gold does for you:

*Focusing on the essence of what you want allows the
creative power of the universe to fill in the blanks.*

Remember how I said I wanted a black 560 SL? Well,
since that time, I moved to Scottsdale, Arizona. It's summer all year long in Scottsdale. This is desert here! And
do you know how steaming HOT a black car gets in the
desert heat after it's been sitting in the sun for a couple
of hours? I literally *thank God* for that gold car. If we had
gotten that black Benz I wanted, I'd be fried by now.

Sometimes, God and the universe have a better idea of
what's right for us than we do. So, give them the space
to help you get what you *truly* want and need. Focusing
on the essence of your Gold lets a creative power a lot
more sophisticated than you or me play a role in our Gold-
getting process.

The Bear Goes Over The Mountain

Remember that kid's song? Okay, so the bear finally makes
it, gets over the mountain, which probably was not all that
easy to do, and the next line is something like, "And what
do you think he saw?"

The other side of the mountain! And you know what's over there? Another mountain.

That's how it is with our Golds.

Just about the time you're going to grab a Gold you've been after ... flash! You see the next mountain. There's always another Gold ... and another and another. So, I suggest you plan for them.

Realize that your Golds will change as you do. They'll get bigger. There'll be different ones—things you can't even imagine wanting right now.

So, make your Golds specific, make them measurable, give them each a "by when"—and leave some room for creativity. Take the time and care to define your Golds in terms of essence, allow them to change with you as you develop and grow—and allow them to grow larger, too!

I said before that a "by when" on your Gold was a tool for you to use. Now, are you ready for this?

Your Golds themselves are just tools.

The truth is, the Golds are not really the point! They're something that you use to get yourself focused and in action. But don't be attached to the tool, to the Gold. Who cares what tool you use to fix your motor? You just care that the motor gets fixed. If it takes a wrench, OK. If it takes a screwdriver, OK. The same thing with Golds. It's not the Golds that are important—it's the results that you are creating ... *and*, enjoying the trip along the way.

Bottom line: Your Golds are a way for you to create the life you're living—and you're always living it *right now*.

Don't Try to Pull Your Horse With a Cart

I often find that people in Network Marketing have the "wrong" Golds.

"Hey, Butwin, who are you to say they're the wrong

Golds for that person?!"

Well, I don't mean "wrong," as in, that's not what the person should want. I mean "wrong," as in, "the cart before the horse."

You see, a lot of people come into Network Marketing focusing first on what they want to *have*. That's the cart—not the horse!

That's why I spoke about habitudes first. Habitudes are about *being*. First you *be*, then you *do*, then you *have*.

Remember, we're human *beings*, not human *doings*.

Being is the horse: it pulls the cart of what you want to *do and have* in your life.

If you are *being* the kind of person who's able to make a fortune in Network Marketing, then you'll *do* the kind of things that person does—and you'll soon find you're *having* the kinds of things a person like that has.

Remember, when you were a kid, the classic Gold-setting question, the one that every kid asks every other kid? It was one of the greatest things we all ever said, and it would be even greater if we kept asking it once we turned adults:

What do you want to be when you grow up?

What a fantastic question! And isn't it interesting that we never said, "What do you want to HAVE when you grow up?" Were we ever smart when we were kids! So, in your Gold-setting process, focus first on this question:

"Who do I want to be?"

. . . and let the do's and have's flow from that. They will.

Gold Requires Digging

Simply put, no digging—no Gold. Without action, no Golds, no check—and no anything else, for that matter!

Golds are tools, tools you use to get into and stay involved in focused action, in the direction and service of the results you want. Golds are like destinations on a road map. Having them turns a Sunday drive into a purposeful journey of productivity and accomplishment. But—and this is the biggest BUT of all:

You MUST take action—DAILY—to achieve your Golds.

Here's something I've found every successful Street Smart Network Marketer knows and does: *He or she works the business every single day!* Take a look at your Golds: there's something you can do every day of your life to move forward toward their accomplishment.

Try this: Take each Gold you have and work it backwards—one step at a time. However big the Gold is, take one step back to see what happened just before you finally achieved the Gold itself . . . then, what happened just before that, and then before that . . . Once you do that, you'll have a sequence of events from today, right now, all the way up to your Gold. And that will provide you with a series of powerful actions you can take that will move you on to achieving your Gold, one simple step at a time.

Let's say your Gold is earning $10,000 a month, and your "by when" is one year from now. Okay, how much will you be making the month before you hit ten grand? $8,500? Okay, and the month before that? . . . and before that?

Then you ask: What actions do I have to take to achieve step one . . . step two . . . etc.? It looks a whole lot easier and more achievable when you break it into bite-sized chunks like this—doesn't it?

Truth is, it not only *looks* that way—it *is* that way.

Another good thing that happens when you do this is that you get to see if your Gold is grounded. If your tracing-it-backwards tells you that your first check needs to be $3,850, and you've never done the business before, and you're currently employed full-time as a hermit ... that's going to be a mighty big stretch for you. You get the picture.

Doing this exercise—tracing your Golds and actions back, one by one, and then taking action each and every day—will ensure your success. No kidding!

If the activity that you're doing is being acted on with correct knowledge, you end up achieving your results! And correct knowledge is simply a matter of knowing your ultimate Gold and what steps are required to get there. That's all.

"What If I'm Not Achieving My Golds?"

Not a bad question.

If you *are* doing all of the things we've talked about so far, and you're *not* achieving the results you want, then probably one of two things is happening.

1) Your activity level is too low, or
2) You're laboring under incorrect knowledge.

Here again, your mentors are the key.

Check with your mentors (upline, sponsors, teachers, etc.) and review what you're doing with both points in mind: ACTIVITY and KNOWLEDGE. Keeping a daily journal of your activities is one key way to help: that way, you and your mentor can easily review what you've done and look for what pieces are missing.

Correcting #2, incorrect knowledge, is the simplest adjustment to make. This is simply what a friend of mine calls a "technical problem": You just need to get the right information and do the right things to get back on track.

Correcting #1, changing your activity level, may be a harder thing to do.

If the amount of action you're taking (or *not* taking!) is the problem, there is usually only one reason for that:

*You don't believe achieving your Gold is possible—
you just don't believe in what you're doing.*

You may *seem* to be lazy, or you may *feel* shy about doing this or that—but really, it all boils down to whether or not you believe that what you're after is possible for you to achieve.

There's no way you will *not* go after what you truly want *if* you think it's possible to have. So if your activity is not up to par, either you don't really want it—or, you don't think you can get it. One of the two will always be true.

What to do?

Ask yourself two questions.

*#1—"If I could have this Gold (whatever it is), right
now, would I take it—yes or no?"*

And look, this isn't a silly question. I mean, do you *really* want the responsibility that comes with earning $1,000,000 a year—the taxes, the financial planning, the investments, people all over you to beg, borrow or *steal* what you've worked so hard to earn? Some people don't!

So, *first* check out whether or not the Gold you've *said* you want is one you *really* want by asking, If I got it, would I accept it?

If your answer is "No," make up a new and better one— a Gold you truly do want.

If your answer is "Yes," great—go for it. But before you do, ask yourself question #2:

#2—"Do I really believe this is possible for me to achieve?"

If you're still with "Yes," then you must commit to doing what it takes to achieve it.

You won't *really* go for anything you don't believe you can have, do, or be. You might go through the motions for a while, but that's all. So, check out your fundamental habitudes of belief once again. If you need to make a change here, you already know how to do that.

And by the way, changing habitudes takes a day-in, day-out effort. That kind of effort is the final key to your success.

One Last Thing You Need

And, oh, what a nasty word it is. *Discipline.*

That's it. Bad news, huh?

Well, no . . . it isn't really. Believe me, I am not "Robert D.-for-Discipline Butwin." The fact is, I got into Network Marketing to be *free*.

Along the way, I learned that some amount of discipline is required. So, I worked to find the most non-disciplined ways of doing discipline I could find. The truth is, you've got to have *some* discipline. What I decided to do was to make it as easy as possible.

That's why I talk about habitudes and Gold-getting the way I do. These are short cuts. Sure, they require time, energy and effort. Like I said, you've got to dig if you want to find Gold. But dig smart—Street Smart!

This book is filled with the Street Smart short cuts I've discovered and others have taught me.

It's true: Discipline is *required*. But *please*, let's make it *no big deal*. Okay?

(I thought you'd agree with me on this one.)

Discipline is easy when you remember what I quoted from Jim Rohn:

"You'll pay the price IF you believe the promise."

Pay the price of discipline now—or pay the price of regret later. It's your choice. Just remember: Discipline weighs ounces—while regret weighs pounds, and can feel like tons!

Chapter Five

"Just Say No"

For years now we've had a national campaign to "Just Say *No* to Drugs." In fact, "Just Say No" has entered our national lexicon as a catch-phrase for exercising good judgment about knowing our limits, and when to steer clear of unwise actions.

Now, as I said earlier, I think we human beings have gotten a bellyful of "No's" in our lives. However, there are certainly times and places where "No" is just the right thing to say.

There are some "No's" needed in your relationship with Network Marketing, too. Actually, there are two kinds of "No's" you'll need to know how and when to say—"No" to some people, and "No" to some situations.

The first kind is what this chapter is about. You've got to learn to say "No" to some people.

Let me tell you a story that illustrates this beautifully.

The Frog and the Scorpion

One lazy, hazy summer afternoon, down on the river bank, two creatures approached each other, a frog and a scorpion. Now, frogs don't care for scorpions, because scorpions sting frogs and kill them. So the frog was naturally very cautious as soon as he saw the scorpion.

But the scorpion *really* wanted to get across the river, and he knew his only chance was to have the frog ferry him over on his back. So, the scorpion was all sweetness and politeness to the frog.

"Hey, friend frog," the scorpion said nicely, "it's a great day to go across to the other side of the river. I know you're a fantastic swimmer. How'd you like to carry me across?"

The frog said, "What—are you crazy? Scorpions sting frogs and we die."

The scorpion replied, "Nah, come on. I wouldn't do *that*. Hey, I want to get across the river . . . and I can't do that if I sting you, right?"

Well, that seemed to make sense, and the frog, being a kind and good-natured fellow, believed the scorpion, allowed him to get up on his back, and headed off across the river, bound for the other side.

About half-way across, sure enough, *Zot!*—the scorpion stung the frog!

As the two of them were about to go under for the third and final time, the frog asked the scorpion, "Why'd you do it—why'd you sting me, after all you said?"

"Hey," said the scorpion, "what can I tell you? . . . I'm a scorpion—and scorpions sting frogs. That's just the way it is."

Why am I telling you this story? I don't want you to get stung!

The point is: If it looks like a duck, and walks like a duck, and quacks like a duck, and water rolls right off its back just like a duck's—*it's a duck!*

Scorpions sting frogs. There are wolves dressed up like sheep. No matter how much you might want it to be otherwise, that's the way it is. Certain people are just the way they are, and they're that way in Network Marketing, too.

There are people to whom you've simply got to say "No" in this business if you want to survive and prosper.

You have to *learn* to recognize these people. You've got to get *seasoned*. That takes time and experience. During that time, and through those experiences, you may get stung a couple of times. Yes, that is one way we human beings learn ... but there are other ways. And one way is to be informed and forewarned.

If It Looks Too Good To Be True ...

... it probably *IS* too good to be true. In other words, it's probably not true!

Here's an easy way to recognize people who aren't for real. From "Get rich quick," to "Sign up with me and I'll build your Network group *for you*," these claims and offers are "Too good to be true." In other words, too bad—*they're false!*

Network Marketing is the freest of all free enterprise, and because of that, it attracts more than its share of flim-flam scam artists. The problem is, there really are people in this business who *did* get rich quick. They are *very* rare, but they have happened. So, many people hang around in the hopes that getting-rich-quick will happen to them, too.

You know the actor Dustin Hoffman? He was an overnight sensation in the movie *The Graduate*. Bingo, one movie—and he was a star, rich, famous, could get any part he wanted ... you know the story.

At least, that's what I thought—until my friend John Kalench pointed out to me that Hoffman was working on Broadway *for over 11 years* before he got his break in *The Graduate*. Sure, he was always a fine actor, but his "big break" came after years and years of hard work and preparation. Maybe you've heard this saying:

Luck is where opportunity meets preparation.

Good expression. Here's another one I like:

More often than not, luck is simply the loser's excuse for the winner's success.

How To Get Lucky

If you want to be lucky in Network Marketing, I'll give you the formula right here and now:

Work your tail off... learn everything you can about this business ... hang out with powerful people who are making it happen ... and, after a couple of years, you WILL get lucky.

Until then, when somebody makes you an offer that sounds too good to be true—refuse.

In conventional small business, the experts say it takes three years to learn about the business, make adjustments in your systems, establish your business and get on solid ground. Why should Network Marketing be any different? It's not.

Here's one of my favorites:

"If you don't get in TODAY, you'll be left behind!"

Nonsense! Amway's been in business for more than 30 years and there are *still* new people on their way to earning big money in Amway. "Sure—but it's harder now than it was in the beginning, right?" Far from it—in fact, the committed people getting in now are reaching the higher achievement levels faster than ever before!

Now, here's the key to discovering when you should say "No":

... Ask the Tough Questions

Probably the best way to find out if someone is a person to whom you should say "No," is to ask those tough questions that reveal the person's true colors. My advice here comes in two parts: First, be *very* direct about what you want to know. And second, get it in writing.

> *"Hey, Bob ... if you sign up with me, in my company, I'll sign up with you in yours. I guarantee you'll make $10,000 in six months. I promise."*

> *"Okay, Jack. I'm all for it. Now, if you'll write that all down in detail on this piece of paper and sign it ... Hey! Where are you going? What's the matter?"*

My friends, if the guy or gal is willing to *promise* you something, ask them to put it in writing. That separates the wheat from the chaff *really* fast!

Sometimes, direct questions can be tough to ask, because they're not always *nice*. And the truth is, most people want other people to think they're *nice*. Forget it! This is your future we're talking about. Ask away!

To: "I'll help you build your business ..."—ask: "Will you give me the names of some of the people you've already done this for, so I can call them and speak with them?"

What if you get a "No" to *that* request—what does that tell you?

Any time someone makes you an offer, you can always ask for References. Asking for referrals from people who've had experience with the person who's offering you a "deal" is a wonderful way to find out the truth. Check them out.

Here are some other things to look for:

People who do not keep their agreements—especially with regard to appointments and doing what they say they're going to do. I'll tell you, people who consistently cannot keep a telephone appointment with you are not very likely to "deliver 10 people to your next meeting"! Not that this necessarily means the person is lying or dishonest. People who say they'll do this or that, and continuously *do not,* may be going through a temporary difficult period in their lives—but if this is their Modus Operandi, stay away from them!

People who lie about their past. There are lots of people in Network Marketing who tell golden tales of how they started as truck drivers or waiters and then earned fortunes in months with their wonderful opportunity. When you check it out, however, you find that they've been successful salesmen for years, or they had successful Networking businesses in another company first. Check them out. In the "straight" business world, it's called doing "due diligence."

People who are overly critical of others—other people, other companies, even other leaders within their own company. If you're on the phone with somebody and she is tearing someone else apart, there's one thing you can be certain of: Sooner or later *you* will be the subject of one of her negative dumps. This is especially true if that person goes out of his or her way to say, "Oh, I don't mean you . . ." or "You're an exception . . ." You can be sure, if someone talks behind someone else's back, they *will* talk behind yours, too.

There's an old sales adage that also fits perfectly for Network Marketing:

Never talk down the competition—you never know when you may be working for them.

The only difference in our business is, you won't be *"working for"* anybody but yourself . . . but the advice is still golden.

Just think what kind of impression you'll make with this position:

"... You know, Jim, the only company and product worth talking about is the one I'm with ... Don't bother looking at the others."

Great! That leaves the rest of the industry looking like a bunch of fools, sharks or snake oil peddlers. Who would want to join an industry like that?

"Nobody?"

Right!

Beware of people who talk down anything or anyone. Talking *up* is the way to go.

People who promise the moon. This is usually done by flashing a big check from the front of the room or across the table in a personal presentation.

"Oh yeah!?!" Have them put it in writing—two ways. First, have them show you, on paper, just how—step-by-step—*you* are going to achieve those marvelous numbers. Then, have them sign a contract. One of those two will usually break the deal, *but*, it'll keep *you* in one piece. Again, do it. Ask them to *show* you how it's done *for real*.

Real leaders—the ones making the *real big* money—know that lasting success in Network Marketing takes hard and smart work, and they have fun doing it—and they'll tell you so.

When President Kennedy promised us the moon, he said it would take us ten years, billions of dollars, and the effort and support of everybody in America. That's called being realistic.

People who make medical claims for products. The law says, you can only make medical claims—i.e., a product cures this or alleviates that—if it's a proven "drug."

Generally, food products, such as herbal drinks or nutritional supplements, and skin care products which are not drugs, according to the FDA, cannot have such curative claims attached to them.

Distributors who tell you a given product cures herpes or cancer are over the edge of the law—*way* over—and you should say "No" to them, big time. If you don't, you and/or your company—*and the entire industry*—could get in real trouble, the least of which is a snug little slam-job segment on "60 Minutes"!

Now, please understand: It's quite true that there are many miraculous products available through Network Marketing—products that do a lot more than you or I are *allowed by law* to say they do. *But* you've got to keep clear of the law! You don't need to be named a co-defendant in a lawsuit between an unhappy consumer (or even a damaged one) and your company. And the truth is, most of these unlawful medical claims come from *distributors*.

Stay clear of all of this. It's not worth the trouble.

Of course, you are allowed to share *your own personal experience* about any product, one-on-one, with anybody. But make sure that's all you do. Our government is quite serious about protecting its citizens from "quack claims"—whether we think they're legitimate or not.

Stay away from claims and be careful when dealing with people who make them. You can easily tell if someone has lost 20 pounds. And you can see the difference in someone who looks 20 years younger than the last time you saw them. Leave it at that.

People who are in someone else's organization—or even deep down on your own fifth or sixth level—who want to sign up with you under a different name. Say NO!!! Nothing, *nothing* cracks the integrity of an organization and a company like this one. What this person is doing is trying to get another line going—under an alias. Chances are quite good that this is a flagrant violation of

the company's "cross-sponsoring" rules and regulations—
and even if that's not spelled out, it certainly violates the
spirit of Networking. So far, I've never seen this done
where bad feelings didn't prevail.

Remember, this is a duplication business. If that one
person does it, what do you think *their* people will tend
to do? Right.

Most companies have a policy to deal with this that
requires a distributor to resign and go through a waiting
period, usually three to 12 months, after which he is free
to sign up with anyone else.

But even doing it the "legal" way is an idea to steer
clear of. There will still be bad feelings—and negative-
word-of-mouth can do a great deal of damage to a Network Marketing company.

People who want you to "front" them products. Now,
you may want to save the world, and you may be the kind
of big-hearted guy or gal whose mission is to uplift people
from their circumstances to a new lease on life. And
Network Marketing is just the vehicle for you to accomplish your mission.

BUT, if a person cannot come up with the minimal amount
of money it takes to get beginning inventory, they are
probably not going to succeed in this business. I have
successful people in my organization who began with one
bottle of product and five tapes.

Sure, that's a tough way to start. You can't sell much
from an empty wagon. But I've also given thousands of
dollars worth of products to people on a promise. Take a
guess at how many of those people ever paid me back . . .
or ever built a business . . .

It's about commitment. If a new distributor comes to
me, and he or she doesn't have the money for initial inventory, and they ask, "Robert, can you help me come up
with ways to start my business with what little I have?"
that's different. I'll work with them like crazy to get them

off on the best foot possible—but not by fronting them product on an open account.

Your company doesn't front *you* product. Neither should you for your distributors. Network Marketing is a cash business. Keep it that way.

Above all, use common sense—which is all too *uncommon* in this day and age.

Trust your intuition. Say "No" to anything or anyone for whom you sense a "No" is appropriate.

Watch for the "deals," such as:

"You sign up with me and I'll sign up with you . . ."

"I'll sign up with you if you kick back 50 percent of the income I earn you per month . . ."

"I'll put people under you—you don't have to work the program at all . . ."

"The levels fill themselves, you don't have to do anything . . ."

All of these are pie-in-the-sky. The people who offer them are scorpions. Remember, scorpions sting frogs, and it's fatal!

That's the people side. The other side of what you've got to say "No" to is some opportunities, and that's what we'll look at next.

CHAPTER SIX

Driving A Hot Set of Wheels

BY "HOT SET OF WHEELS," I DON'T MEAN A STOLEN CAR. DON Failla was the first person I'm aware of to refer to the Network Marketing company or opportunity you become affiliated with as your "vehicle."

It's a perfect analogy in many ways. The Network Marketing company you choose to represent is your vehicle. If you've gotten a good one, you should be able to hop in, turn the key and drive off in your new business vehicle down the highway of success.

So when you go looking for the right opportunity, use the same caution that you'd use when you're buying a car. Some Networking vehicles are Porsches. Some are Mercedes. And some are 32 Ford Deuce Coupe hot rods with blown engines—they look fast, but you'll have to replace the engine before you can even take it around the block.

Some Networking vehicles are race cars—and others are absolute Yugos!

The trick is, how to pick the best vehicle *for you*. Preferably, it should be a hot set of wheels that's fun to drive *and* safe, dependable transportation to your future success.

The Two Kinds of Vehicles

There are two very different types of opportunities that call themselves Network Marketing companies: the Direct Sales companies and the Multi-Level companies.

Direct Sales Companies

Direct Sales companies are known as "seller-based," which means that they give more income to the distributor when he or she makes a sale at retail. These vehicles usually market higher-ticket, one-time-sale, durable items such as air and water filters, durable automotive products, higher-priced memberships, etc.

The value of these types of opportunities is that every time you make a sale, you earn more *per* sale. So, you earn more money faster.

Successful direct sales people are *salespeople*. They're paid based on how much they individually sell, so they try to sell lots and lots! Their main focus is on making sales, not on building a Network organization of lots of people who are taught to sell a little bit each.

If you're a super-sales type, this may be good news for you. However, it limits the number of people you can bring into the business with you to those who are sales types just like you. And that can be bad news.

There's more bad news: Direct sales vehicles cost more to get involved with, because you've got to invest more in initial inventory, and because each individual unit of product costs more. This also may be a barrier for other people you're bringing into the business with you, because it costs so much more for *them* to start. And one other down-side is that there usually is little or no *residual income.*

What's "residual income"? That's income you earn from

your initial efforts that continues to generate earnings for you long after your day-to-day attention to the "sale" or to your business. The "royalties" a writer or performing artist makes on their creation is an example of residual income; so is the interest earned on a stock investment. Residual income is a feature of "Multi-Level" or Networking companies with consumable, repeat-purchase products.

Multi-Level Companies

Multi-Level companies usually offer reasonably priced (i.e., not "high-ticket") products that people consume within a month or two and then re-order.

You'll earn less money up-front with a consumable—the retail profit on a $15 bottle of a consumable product is much less than the $60 to $100 you might earn on a high-ticket item, such as an air filter or water filter. But if the product is really great, and people love it and depend on it—such as with a great nutritional supplement or super skin care item—they'll buy it again and again, sometimes for years and years and years.

It's easier to attract people to this kind of opportunity for a number of reasons:

1) It costs less to get involved. A few hundred dollars of initial inventory will usually cover all but the most aggressive beginning distributor's needs. And that means . . .

2) More people are able to *become* involved, another plus. What's more . . .

3) There's residual income.

To be fair, some high-ticket, durable products, like air and water filters, need replacement filters, and that provides some residual earning benefit. And some of these devices must be replaced in three or four years, so there's a potential repeat purchase off in the distance, too. But real, consistent residual income comes from a product or product line that people use up and re-order every month or two.

There are some Network Marketing companies offering products that I'll use for the rest of my life. Just think about the value of my purchases to the distributor who sold them to me—or who sponsored me! And just think about having a distributor Network of 1,000 people, each of whom orders $50 worth of products every month for their own personal use! 1,000 x $50 is $50,000 of product sales volume each month. And if you make, say, 10 percent of that ... Well, you can figure it out.

And finally, a fourth point:

4) Multi-Level Networks are built by a lot of people, each doing a little bit.

Direct Sales *requires* a *salesperson* to make it work. And the truth is, most people *hate* the idea that they're going to "sell."

Of course, the fact is that Network Marketing *is a sales and distribution business*. No matter what we may want to say about it, sales is involved.

The difference between our industry and others is *how* we "sell." And this especially applies to consumable-product companies.

"Hard sell" is out in Network Marketing. "Soft sell" is in. We simply recommend products or services we think are great—and people either get them or they don't.

It's just like reading a great book, seeing a wonderful movie, discovering a fabulous restaurant, or listening to a terrific tape. You get excited about it and you tell your friends. They either follow your lead and try it—or they don't. No big deal.

And that's just what we do, and how we do it, in Network Marketing.

Since you only need a few people to try the products

along with you—because you're building an organization where everyone's doing the same thing—there isn't the pressure for you personally to perform a large volume of sales. Remember, Network Marketing is *a lot of people each doing a little bit*. That's why it is that you can build a Network with monthly total sales volume of staggering proportions—and receive a whopping big check!

Of course, this makes it much easier to attract people to join you in the business. Since they don't "have to sell" and they can simply make recommendations through word-of-mouth to people they already know, it's a far less threatening business than one where you have to become a salesperson and move a lot of product.

Now let's look at some criteria for selecting this vehicle of yours.

How To Choose The Best Vehicle For You

Once you've decided which of the two kinds of products or services and companies you want to work with, what about the specific opportunity you're looking at? What considerations do you have as to whether or not this is the one you want?

Here's a quick checklist of what to look for. (Many people contributed to this list: Corey Augenstein, Keith Laggos, David Stewart, Debbi Ballard, Burke Hedges, Kent Ponder, Mike Sheffield, and others.)

1. What's the Value of the Product or Service? You've got to choose a vehicle with a product you like—*A LOT*.

Because we are a word-of-mouth marketing business, you've got to have good-to-great things to say about your products. The most successful people I know in Network Marketing are people who *love* their products.

The best advice here is to choose a vehicle with products that you're proud of. Nothing takes the place of this.

79

You've got to be a product of your product.

Apply all the same criteria to your potential product or service as you would to any other offering in any other marketplace. Does it represent real value? Is there a continuing demand for it? Is it unique—i.e., is there nothing else like it available from stores or through the mail? Does it get results for people?

Make sure you've got a "fit" with these questions before you commit to the opportunity.

2. Does It Have Integrity? Now here's something you can't fake! The products, people, company, literature, all MUST have integrity. If not—*do not get involved.*

How can you tell? Same way as you did with people: Check them out. Look for companies and upline distributors doing what they said they'd do . . . no lies or outrageous exaggerations . . . a history of commission checks on time and accurate . . . standing behind the product and the compensation plan . . . treating distributors fairly . . . all that kind of stuff.

Ask your questions directly to the company, to your potential sponsor—and to other distributors, too. This takes a little homework—but it's worth it.

Of course, just because you hear a discouraging word or two, don't take it as the whole truth and nothing but the truth. Make sure you see for yourself.

Just know this: Without integrity—there is no hope of success.

Here is one of the many terrific things Venus Andrecht says in her superb book, *MLM Magic—How An Ordinary Person Can Build An Extraordinary Networking Business From Scratch:*

"This business either builds character—or exposes it." *Excellent!*

3. Is the Company "Distributor-Driven"? This is a term

I first saw David Stewart use in an article in the *Upline*™ Journal. It means that the Networking company you're looking at makes all of its business decisions with the distributors in mind. It's called "The Distributor Comes First," and it's one of those MUST's for a successful Network Marketing company.

Sure, I can hear all you corporate and Country Club Smart people saying, "Yeah, but if the company doesn't make a profit, *there will be no* distributors." True enough. And just who is it that generates all that profit? The distributors in the field. This entire business revolves around *us*. It is very accurate to say that in Network Marketing, distributors are where the power is.

Okay, so how can you tell whether or not a company knows this and lives and works by it?

First, they never *ever* say, or act, or even *seem* to act, like this is *their* business. It's ours, yours and mine. The business card reads "Robert Butwin's Such & Such Company Business . . ." or "Robert Butwin, Independent Distributor for Such & Such." Beware the company President who comes on the training video saying anything different!

Company CEO's (and their entire companies, staff and stockholders) need to hold distributors as their business partners. There are some who think distributors are a necessary evil. *Stay away from those guys!!!* They'll be out of business before *they* know it.

Look at the company's support materials—all the sales, product and compensation manuals and brochures. Are they made *for* you? Do they all make it easier *for you* to do the business? If not—look out.

And here's a pet peeve of mine: over-priced sales support!

Now, I'm a business person and I'm all for profit centers. But it's the distributors who are *the* profit centers for a Networking company. A company that offers videos, audios and other sales and training aids as inexpensively as possible, priced solely to recover their costs of creation and production over a reasonable period of time, is on track. They will have more profit centers than a company intent on having that slick new video make a $200,000 profit.

I heard a rumor once that one particular flashy, explosive new Networking company sold $20 million in videos in their first year! Wow! Great profit center. And I hope it's at least partially true, for their sake—because that company never saw year one-and-a-half.

So, look at the company's systems. Especially look in two areas: distributor training and distributor services.

The golden hallmark of a good-to-great Network Marketing company is excellent field training and support. Regularly scheduled, company-sponsored schools and events around the country. A "customer service" department that excels. (And remember who the company's customer is— the folks who buy the products? No: The folks who distribute them and sponsor others who do the same ... that's you!)

Again, you can best check out both of these areas of the company by speaking with both long-time and brand-new distributors. See what kind of training they've received and what kind of service they get from the company. A good company-opportunity-vehicle is like an excellent car dealer: The best have award-winning service departments.

Look For A Duplicatable Business System

One more system that's vitally important—but missing in most Networking companies—is a duplicatable business system. Most companies leave this up to the distributors themselves. They say things like:

"It's your business. We leave you free to create it any way you choose."

Doesn't that sound great? Well, it's not! It's lazy and

irresponsible.

Harsh words? Yes. But there *are* Network Marketing companies, few and far between, who see this as *their* responsibility.

They offer their distributors an easily duplicatable business development system that anyone could use his first day in the business. In some cases, you might find that while the company itself doesn't have a system like this, an upline organization or Distributor Association does. Either way—look for it.

A ready-made, duplicatable business-building system is an absolute Godsend! When you find a company that gives you a booklet or video with "10 Steps To Building A Successful Business," or "The Five-Point-Plan For Your Success"—you've got a serious company! Chances are they know what you need to succeed. They've been where you are and have gone to great lengths to stack the odds for success in your favor, because that's what they've found works best. They're serious about helping you create success and build a profitable business. They're very good!

Most important of all, they know how vital and important your success is *for them.* Yes, we're all in this for ourselves; companies, too. The difference between the good guys and the not-so-good guys is *how* they do it. As a Network Marketing distributor, you have the right to expect them to *Do It All For You.*

Please, I'm not saying ". . . do *YOUR* work *for* you." No way! But as noted author and financial guru Charles Givens points out, 80 percent of every successful company's efforts is *marketing.* And since, in Network Marketing, you and I (the distributors) are the ones doing that 80 percent of the work, we deserve all the support our company can muster!

4. Does It Have Good Management? Yes, just the same as with any traditional business, good management is a must. And in this business, management with Network

Marketing experience is a must, too—a super-must!

I've seen lots of smart corporate cookies and enlightened entrepreneurs come and go in this business fast! Why? They didn't understand what they were doing.

It's a rare person who can come into Network Marketing and attain any real mastery of this business—who hasn't been out on the street and worked it. True, you don't have to be a chicken to know all you need to know about an egg. And you don't have to be a computer programmer to make a PC sing to your command. But in Network Marketing, if you aren't a seasoned pro, you'd better hire a few or move in with some if you're going to run a successful Network Marketing company.

I *always* look for experienced Networkers *with integrity*. If there's a questionable man or woman high up in the company, *don't touch it!* One bad apple *will* spoil the whole bunch. Sometimes, people like this finagle their way up into the company and eventually get found out—and spit out. Here's the problem: Are you willing to wait for this natural process to come full circle—and can you afford to hang around for the months or even years it takes to clean up the mess they leave? My answer is "No" to both.

What else?

Avoid those companies that make sweetheart deals with "heavy hitters." That's the one where Harry Heavy promises to come over with his entire "monster" downline *if* the company inserts him first level ... then creates six new levels above him that he can sell to even bigger heavy hitters from other programs ... and promises to give him $100,000 to tide him over till all of his people sign up.

Guess what? He'll be gone when the first *better* deal comes along, leaving behind him a crippled company—one you'll be very sorry you're with.

"Deals *rarely* work"—and this heavy hitter example is the rarest of all. Harry Heavy is the only one who makes money. There's no loyalty in wheeler-dealers—and without loyalty, the kind that comes from helping people become successful by teaching and training them to build a prosperous Network, there's no longevity in Network Marketing. And that spells death for the distributor who's worked hard for a *residual* income.

5. Does It Have a Fair, Just and *Juicy* Compensation Plan? Here's the A-Number-One cautionary point (and here's a bit of my country club past showing through): Look out for sand traps!

Sand traps?! Yes: There are compensation plans that trap you by taking people away just when you've made it big, or raising the group volume requirement (all the sales made by you and your Network group of distributors) to a point so high, not even the Hunt brothers in their heyday could hit it with a pound of silver. BEWARE!

The problem for newcomers is that often they don't have the knowledge to evaluate whether the compensation plan is legitimate or not.

Time for mentoring—get someone experienced in mentoring or coaching to take a look for you and with you. And again, the best advice is to go step by step through the plan with *your* specific and unique scenario figured out in time, energy and dollars.

Some plans are top-heavy—they reward the big guys at the top in a big way, and make it tough on all the little guys (who, by the way, *always* make up around 80 percent *or more* of the participation in any Network Marketing company).

Some plans are bottom-heavy—they pay beginners the lion's share and take that cash from the real business-builders. When this happens, you've either got no real leaders, or leaders who don't like being leaders in this opportunity, which is worse than having none at all.

So, a balanced compensation plan is a must. Get someone who knows to help you check it out. If you don't have such a person, call one of the industry trade papers or magazines and ask them whom to ask.

Here's a shotgun list of do's and don't's.

DON'T mess with a company that's changed its compensation plan thirteen times in the last two years. They're either stupid, crooked or both.

Changes *are* needed. Plans evolve. But good companies make fundamental adjustments few and far between, and when they do, they spend months asking the distributors for feedback *before* they make change number one.

DO work with companies that have had some difficult times in the past—whether it's financial, legal, whatever—and have come through them. These guys know what tough times are like and how to get through them. If the company you're in or are interested in has met the challenges and emerged from them in one piece, you've got a strong bet that they're in it for the long term.

Don't be afraid of companies with a past—as long as they're better today than ever before.

DON'T be seduced by cruises, vacations, conventions, travel prizes and the like. My wife Bonnie and I have been on enough cruises. Now, we'd rather stay home and earn money! *Really.*

Now, one goodie I *do* like is a car allowance. It's a great incentive and an even greater reward. What's more, it really keeps leaders in the game and productive. After all, who wants to give up her car just because the sales volume was too low for three months in a row? Nobody. But for me, you can keep the boat ride to Cancun. I'll take mine in cash and go where I want, when I want, and take the kids because I want to.

DON'T buy into *anything* with wild or crazy income claims. Do your own due diligence and make sure you know exactly how the particular program will work *for you.* The Networking graveyard is filled with people who didn't earn

$10,000 their first month in the business—but planned and spent like they did.

If there's a guy on stage telling you he made $46,000 his third month in the business and *you will too*, stand up ... and walk out!

DO shop around—and not just for a vehicle (company/opportunity), but for a sponsor, too. There's no law that requires you to sign up with the first person you talk to about this or that opportunity. Your sponsor is someone you've got to trust, have some chemistry with, and who's willing to make a commitment to your success. If the person you're speaking with isn't all of that, look for someone else.

Also, remember, it's not just that one individual with whom you're signing up. It's his upline organization, as well. There are Network groups in every program that are really hot and really doing the business. Being part of that kind of dynamic group effort puts the odds for success more in your favor. Instant momentum!

So, don't be afraid to shop for a vehicle and a sponsor—one you get along with well and who has a strong upline.

You've heard the three top rules for successful real estate: "Location ... location ... location ..." Well, in Network Marketing it's about the same. It's "vehicle and sponsor ... vehicle and sponsor ... vehicle and sponsor." They're both critical.

What else?

You'll pick up more ideas from some of the next couple of chapters, but all the above will give you a great start on selecting the proper vehicle for yourself.

Remember, there are no guarantees. You can choose the perfect vehicle and still have an accident. You can drive it around a while and discover it's not *really* what you wanted. Sad but true, sometimes the only way to know what a vehicle is like is to drive it for a few months. And every once in a while people get a lemon. Life is like that.

No matter what, the bottom line is *you*. Even if you do choose a vehicle that's not perfect, make sure you come out of it better, smarter, more able and more capable than when you went in. There are lots of successful people in Network Marketing who learned their stuff with one company, then moved on, and made it big with the second one. Now, I'm not suggesting you swap vehicle after vehicle, hoping to get the one that makes you rich. The point I'm making is this: Your success in this business boils down to *you*.

I've known several people who've become so good in this business, they can go with almost *any* vehicle and be winners. It pays—and can pay big—to get the very best vehicle for you that you possibly can, but again, in the end, your success depends on you.

What I want to cover in the next couple of chapters are some things that will help you get the street smarts you need to make it—anywhere, anytime and with any company you want.

As Stephen Covey points out in his great book, *The Seven Habits of Highly Effective People*, we progress from dependence, to independence, to interdependence. It's great to create your independence, to know that *you* can make it *anywhere*. It's even greater to know that—*and* to be working with a truly great company and sponsor!

Next, let's take a closer look at creating your independence—and financial independence.

CHAPTER SEVEN

Where the Action Is

I COULD AS EASILY HAVE CALLED THIS CHAPTER "WHEN THE Action Is," because the action happens once you are in a place—where—and at a point in time *WHEN* you gain the understanding of what this Network Marketing business is really all about.

I've met people who've been in this business for years and still have no real idea what Network Marketing is all about. I've also met a few people who achieved a genuine understanding of Network Marketing within their first few days. And I do mean *a few.*

The truth is, I don't know how to have someone *understand* anything—much less this unconventional business of ours. There's no formula to follow or magic pill to take. What's more, gaining that understanding seems to involve different requirements for different people.

How Do You Ride A Bicycle?

It's like riding a bicycle.

How do you get someone to "understand" how to ride a bicycle?

Well, you can tell people all about bicycles . . . all about their design and how they work. You can tell them all about how to ride one, and explain what it's going to be like. You can even show them a video that shows all that in detail.

And after all that, will they "know how" to ride one—will they actually *be able to do it?* No way!

Until they actually get on and try it—ride and fall, again and again, and finally ride off down the street—there's no way they'll ever truly *understand* what it is!

Network Marketing is just like that. Until you actually get on and ride it, there's no way you'll really *understand* what it's like.

So, why bother reading this book?

Good question.

What I'm doing is *preparing you to gain understanding.*

No, this book won't do it all for you, nor will any other book or tape or seminar. Understanding Network Marketing is a *proactive process* in which your *doing the business* is the only way to truly learn, develop and grow.

So what *will* this book do? It will tell you "where the action is."

So, let's hit some fundamentals.

The Difference Between Addition and Multiplication

Don Failla points this out in his book, *How To Build A Large Successful Multi-Level Marketing Organization.* This is so important because multiplication is what builds momentum in this business. If you don't have multiplication, if your growth is merely additive, you'll either burn out, accomplish nothing—or both.

Addition—at least in business—is *hard* work.

Multiplication is *smart* work.

Have you ever seen the classic plate-spinning act? A guy comes out on stage and gets a row of eight or nine plates spinning up on the ends of five- or six-foot long poles. This is amazing to watch: He gets the first one going

... then the second ... then the third ... then the fourth ... and by then he's got to run back to the first one to keep it spinning so it won't fall and break. Then he restarts the second ... then the third ... and so on throughout the act.

He runs back and forth, back and forth, and each time he gets a new one going, he has to run back and restart all the others all over again. It's an endless process of trying to keep them all spinning in the air at one time. The audience laughs and claps—and the truth is, that guy has picked one wicked crazy way to earn a living!

And you know what? That's just what the majority of Network Marketers do. They "get people going" like spinning plates on the ends of sticks. Talk about a balancing act!

This business isn't about spinning all those plates. And it's not about trying to sign up everybody you know or have ever known. It's not *addition*.

Network Marketing is about uncovering leaders who will duplicate themselves and *multiply* their efforts (and yours) throughout their entire organization—which is also *your* organization.

Once you create multiplication in your business-building, you don't have to run back to the first one, the second and so on. The growth of your organization becomes self-sustaining.

Five Times Five Times Five ...

Five is really *the* magic number in our business.

This is similar to a military model, which discovered that the optimal utilization of staff officers occurred with groups of five. In Network Marketing, five is also the optimal number of key first level leaders. Show me a successful "Heavy Hitter" and I'll show you a person with close to 90 percent—or more—of his or her monthly commission check coming from *two to five downline legs each headed by one key leader* (or key leader couple).

91

The truth is, in Network Marketing you DON'T build an organization of hundreds and thousands of people—at least not personally. What you do is build an organization of *ones and tens* of people, among whom will be TWO TO FIVE key leaders who will do the same thing—and that's where the hundreds and thousands come from!

Armed with that information, set your goal of finding five people who want to build a business just like you do, and "move in" with them (as Tom Schreiter puts it)—train, teach and support them as if it were the only thing in your business life there is to do. Because you know what? *It is!*

Understanding How To Make Money

Okay, right up front—only the government and counterfeiters *make* money. Most of us have to *earn* it. So how do you earn money in Network Marketing?

There are three ways: (1) Retail, (2) Referral Marketing, and (3) Network-Building. We'll look at each in turn.

First, retail.

Retail profits are a viable way to earn money in this business. Lots of people do. It's also, as Sandy Elsberg says, "Right Now Money . . ." cash in hand . . . C.O.D. . . . and that's always good. BUT, there are shortcomings in a retail-based Networking business.

For one thing, a whopping majority of our population has a negative image of sales of any kind. Everybody in North America has been sold something that didn't live up to the expectations fostered by the salesperson. We've all been sold something at some time that we didn't want, didn't need, or that didn't work. That's why so many of us have such a dim view of sales and salespeople.

Want to push someone's buttons? Ask them to go *sell* something. That'll do it. The funny thing about that is that when you do, the person will spend the next fifteen or twenty minutes passionately and persuasively convincing you *"They can't sell!"* And they'll do such a good job that you'll be ... well, sold!

If you want to have some real fun with them, after they're finished with their emotional "I can't sell" rap 'n' routine, hold up your hand and say, "Okay, okay ... I got it. You've sure *sold* me!" They might just get it—and realize that in truth, we're all selling *what we believe in* all the time.

You know, it's crazy—but it's true: In America, the greatest consumer society in the entire world, nobody wants to sell. (Which is why top sales producers in any business earn incredible incomes.)

Anyway, if your business is retail-based—that is, if the retail sale is the focus of what you do—you're facing an uphill battle when it comes to having people join you in your *selling* business. It's clearly the wrong message to send when your goal is to build a large organization made up of people *who won't sell!*

You only get one chance to make a first impression, and when your first impression is that Network Marketing is all about *sales*, you're making building your business an uphill battle.

Now, the truth is that we *all* sell all the time. The question is, in Network Marketing, what are you *really* selling?

What Are You *Really* Selling?

The first and most important thing you are selling in Network Marketing is—*yourself.*

People will not look at the material you're presenting, and won't even hear what you're saying, if they do not immediately perceive that you are sincere and concerned about them ... if they do not sense that you have their best interests at heart ... if they do not *buy you* first.

You know how long it takes for people to make a buying decision in a television commercial? *Four seconds—max!*

How about a print advertisement in a newspaper or

magazine? 75 percent of them do their buying *in the headlines alone!*

How about a live sales presentation? Do you have a 20-minute presentation, or a 45-minute interview? Well, guess what?—your prospect made up his or her mind within the *first three minutes!*

These are scientifically proven figures. Most "buying decisions" are made immediately and unconsciously. They are based on emotion, not on thought. We have a matter of minutes (*at most*) to *sell* ourselves in an encounter with a new person. What we do and say the rest of the time is actually "post-selling," that is, giving our customer or prospect added factual "ammunition" and reinforcement to *support* their already-made emotional choice.

Positioning Yourself

Do you remember that television commercial with tennis star André Agassi—the one that flashes all these different pictures, one after the other, ending with André pulling down his sunglasses and saying, "Image is everything"?

It's very important to position your image. By "image," I don't mean making something appear different than what it really is, or being phony. I mean—what key message do you want to send about who you are and what you're up to?

Remember, you're selling yourself.

In fact, *you* may be the *only* thing you sell, if you approach your business the way I do. Almost everything else I do, I do *through tools*—brochures, tapes and the rest. I let the tools do the work . . . In other words, I let them do *their* work—so I can focus on doing *my* work.

What's "my work"? It's creating trust and rapport with people—selling them on myself and on my value to them as a sponsor and mentor. I work on that—and let the tools do the work of selling the Network Marketing opportunity, the products and the company.

Since you're always selling yourself, I believe the best way to do that is to have a piece *about yourself* to give your prospects. Third-party endorsements are the best, and what better way than to have such an endorsement written for you?

I've been interviewed in *Upline*™, and I show all my prospects a reprint of that article. It's a highly respected publication, nicely typeset, it's impressive, and it does the job.

"But Robert, Upline™ *hasn't interviewed me."*

That's okay. There are hundreds of free-lance writers around who *can* interview you for a very reasonable price. Do you live near a college with an English or Journalism department? Put an ad up on their bulletin board with your phone number on it. College kids always need extra cash. (And after they write up your interview, get them into your business!)

After you get the transcript (and a 5 x 7 black and white glossy photo of you looking terrific), edit it so it's what you want, then thumb through the Yellow Pages and find a "desktop publisher" or print shop (the desktop guys are usually cheaper) and have them typeset your interview so it looks exactly like a page from *Inc., Forbes, People* or *Upline*™. Then print up a few hundred.

Instant fame and recognition.

"Naw, that's cheating."

No way! It's working smart. Just make sure the article says what you want it to, and that it tells the truth—and you've made yourself a *position*. It's another tool. Give a copy to every one of your prospects.

You Are Your Business

You *are not* selling your products and you *are not* selling your company. Your prospects are not going to work *with* Cell Tech, Light Force, Natural World, Oxyfresh, etc. (If they want to do that, they can apply for a job in the corporate offices.) They are going to work in your organization *with you!* What you *are* selling them is the fact that *you've got* the insight, skills and knowledge to help them develop a successful career.

I'd like to dispel an old myth, the one that goes, "What you don't know won't hurt you." That's totally erroneous! But what you *do know* will make a tremendous difference, especially in your business, because *you are* your business.

We attract the wealth we want in our lives—and the people we want in our business—by who we are and what we are up to. Who we are and what we're doing is a product of the knowledge we have and continue to gain—and, that we *let other people know* we have to offer them.

What you know makes a big difference in *your value*, and that's important because *you* are your business. That's what people are "buying" when they sign up with you in your Network Marketing business.

Adding To Your Value

I mentioned that I was interviewed in *Upline*™—and truth is, interview or not, *Upline*™ is a super-valuable tool for you, too.

Upline™ contains the kind of knowledge that will *increase your value*, and therefore the value of your business. Besides the informative articles, interviews and Resource Catalog (where you can get books and tapes at a discount), and in addition to the free book they give you when you subscribe, there's one super way *Upline*™ adds to your value.

In their "Editorial Policy" on page 2 of every issue, here's what it says:

What that means is that every article you find, in any issue, can be copied and sent to your retail customers, prospects and downline people.

Remember—*let the tools do the selling*. And *Upline™* is one of the most versatile and powerful tools I have. I am forever photocopying interviews and articles and using them in my prospecting and training. That way, I've got all of the newsletter's knowledge as part of *my* value—the value of my business.

The System Is The Solution

Now, as I said before, most people do not like to "sell"— that is, they don't like the *idea* that they're going to "sell." The best way to deal with that stigma is right up front in your presentation.

As I said earlier, this is a business with "a lot of people each doing a little." Put another way, you don't "sell" in the way we usually think of it. What you're really selling is an intangible—a *promise*. It's the promise that you've got the skill, the knowledge, to help people create the lifestyle they've always dreamed of.

You're in the *lifestyle development business*—not sales. And as such, you've got a system you can teach to others which will enable them to own their own life. You've got a system they can use to build their own business. It's duplicatable. And when they learn how to use it and practice enough to get good at it, they can turn around and do that with other people.

What we're all really selling is the lifestyle possible in Network Marketing—and the fact that we know how to impart access to that lifestyle. You are your *real* product.

And as every savvy marketer knows, making constant improvements in the product is the way to keep one step ahead of the competition.

The Question of Sales and Selling

There's a question I like to ask when I'm giving seminars, and whenever I do, I *always* get a unanimous "Yes!" Here's the question:

> *Have you ever felt taken advantage of, at least once in your life, in the sales process?*

Everyone has had that experience—and because of that, it's key that you reframe the whole issue of sales and selling, so that people can get a clear picture of what this business is really all about. And I don't know of anybody who has said this better than Russ DeVan, so I've gotten Russ' permission to reprint in full an article he wrote on the subject for *Upline*™ magazine. Here's what Russ wrote:

Don't like "selling?" There's a better way—and the good news is, you're already very good at it.

Sales and selling as we know it are uncomfortable for a great many people. In Network Marketing, a business powered by duplication, we've got to develop a simple easy system to accomplish sales that nearly everyone can do. If people are uncomfortable with something, they won't do it.

That's why we need an alternative to traditional sales.

It's not that selling is bad. Developing sales skills can be very useful. But the sales process itself—learning closes, handling objections, distinguishing features, advantages and benefits—is too hard for most people.

Buying is one thing. Being sold is another. Selling tends to be manipulative and people have a built-in resistance to being pushed or pulled to do things.

People love to purchase, but hate to be sold. There's another way to accomplish the goal of sales without the old paradigm conflict of buying and selling.

It's called *promoting*.

When you're selling, the result you're after is *to get the order*. When you're promoting, the result is *to successfully communicate value*. Do you see the difference? When you're promoting, your job is done once people understand the value of what you're offering.

Selling is a learned technique. You're not born a sales person, it's something you become after studying and developing the use of the tools and techniques of the trade. *But you are a born promoter*. We all are.

Think of something you're excited about. Did you read *Men Are From Mars, Women Are from Venus* and think it was great? Did you love the movie *Forrest Gump?* Is there a car that turns you on? . . . a restaurant with great food you enjoy?

When people get excited about something, we have a natural commitment to share that with somebody else. The more valuable the product or experience, the more committed we are to telling other people about it.

The Japanese have a word for this—*giri*. It means *obligation*. The wisdom behind it is that once you've been given something of value and from which you get benefit, you're *obligated* to return the favor, to give it away to other people.

This sharing of your enthusiasm I call *promoting*. It's not sales *per se*—but a lot of things get sold by people promoting them. In fact, it's the way most things "get sold."

I made a movie and I know film companies and producers count on word of mouth to sell tickets. That's promotion—and it's a more powerful and effective "sales" method than advertising or previews in getting people into theaters.

When *Jurassic Park* came out, it was promoted for a short time with advertising. People went to see it. Those people came away from the movie jumping up and down: "You gotta' see this! This movie is incredible! There's a Tyrannosaurus Rex that eats this lawyer who's hiding in an outhouse ..." Remember?

As a result of that initial response, the film company *stopped all their advertising*! *Jurassic Park* is the most successful movie of all time—over $750 million in sales worldwide. By the end of 1995, it was estimated that over two billion people—*two fifths of the world*—had seen that movie!

But when was the last time you saw it advertised?

The ad budget for Arnold Schwarzenegger's *Last Action Hero* was *much* bigger than *Jurassic Park's*, but it was a box office disaster! Why? People didn't promote it. Well actually they did—they promoted the rest of us *not* going to see it.

We promote all the time.

In Network Marketing, as soon as people get caught up in the process of selling, they lose their ability to promote effectively. The more people get into having to sell, trying to sell, the further they get from the natural, contagious enthusiasm of promoting.

Imagine taking a course on "How to sell people on going to see *Jurassic Park.*" First, you'd learn how to qualify your prospects, the pre-approach steps, how to initiate a conversation, build rapport, discover their needs and wants as far as entertainment is concerned. You'd get trained on how to distinguish the film's features from its benefits, how to lead with those benefits and weave them into an effective presentation. The course teaches you how, when the prospect says something negative, you go positive; when she's positive, you go negative with a "take away." You practice handling a series of common objections and learn how to overcome each of them. You're given a script to follow. You learn the Assumptive close, the Ben Franklin close, the Colombo close.

Now, go sell somebody on going to that movie.

Do you see the dramatic difference between selling and promoting? Do you like to sell? Do you like to be thought of as a salesperson? When people ask you what you do, do you say, "I'm in sales?" How many men and women in your organization think of themselves as sales people?

Some people are great at sales. Most people aren't. But most people *are* great promoters. Watch children when they want something.

Which is easier to duplicate: sales or promoting?

When you're selling, the issue is you as a salesperson. When you're promoting, what's important is the value of what you're offering.

With sales, the messenger and his or her ability to sell is the bottom line. With promoting, it's the message—not the messenger.

When you sell, you have to be a good salesperson. When you promote, all you have to be is excited about what you're talking about. The prospect isn't judging your sales ability. He's judging the value of the product you're so enthusiastic about *for himself.*

When you're selling, it's about you. It's personal. If they say "No," they're saying "No" to you *personally.* They're rejecting you, because sales is about *you* getting them to buy what you're selling.

When you're promoting, it's about them. It's personal all right — *for them.* If they say "No," *they* say "No" for *themselves*—not for you.

In sales, you want them to give *you* something—the order. In promoting, you want to give *them* something— the value.

Sales is *taking.* Promoting is *giving.*

When you want something and somebody says "No," how do you feel?

When you give something to somebody and they refuse the gift, how do you feel? You may be disappointed, but it's their loss isn't it? *Next . . . .*

Promoting starts with recognizing the value for your-self. What's the value of your product *for you?* What's the real value of the opportunity *for you?*

Ask yourself: What has this product done for me? What benefits have I gotten from using these products? How have they contributed to me? . . . changed me for the better? . . . made a positive difference in my life?

Ask yourself about your opportunity: How has being involved made my life better, more fun, more exciting? What new things have I learned? What new skills have I developed? How has my opportunity contributed to my life . . . to my family and friends? What are the possibilities for my future?

Then, share that. That's your *Jurassic Park.*

Instead of counting how many retail sales you've made this week, count the number of people you've told about your products. Instead of counting how many prospects you've signed up, count the number of times you've enthu-siastically shared your opportunity.

That's what really *counts.*

Earning Money By Referral Marketing

"Referral Marketing" is when you refer someone to a new and better way of doing things. In our case, we refer people to how they can become a "smart consumer" by purchas-ing valuable products they use and enjoy at wholesale, buying direct from the company, instead of paying the full retail price.

Do you know anybody who doesn't want to save money buying wholesale? You can save $2000 to $12,000 *and more* buying your next car wholesale. From office supplies to clothing and shoes, to just about anything, buying direct from the manufacturer can save you a bundle. Plus, what about the convenience of to-your-door delivery? Forget "one-stop shopping"—this is no-stop shopping!

Network Marketing companies offer smart consumers a

perfect way to get substantial discounts, in-home shopping and delivery to their door. They get all of this by signing up as distributors.

They do that because *you referred them*. And because you referred them, the company will pay you a small commission on everything they buy for as long as they're buying it.

They save money and time and get added convenience— you get a piece of the action. Classic win-win scenario. (And of course the company wins, too: win-win-win.)

All it costs the smart consumer is the distributor application fee (if any), which he or she will make back, usually on the very first order they place. All it costs you is your time and keeping in touch with them, giving them news about the company and products they might have overlooked (remember, they get all the newsletters, new product info, and other benefits you get as a distributor, too).

Next, you move smart consumers up and into the business by showing them how they can get their products for free simply by recommending them successfully to others.

This is something, of course, that we all do all the time— except usually we don't get paid for it. And that concept alone is enough to have a smart consumer become a distributor, especially when he or she has been using the product for a couple of weeks or months and has already "sold" enough to interested family and friends.

From there, it's a short hop to showing how, in addition to getting their product for free, they can make a car payment, chop down a credit card bill or even make a mortgage payment by simply devoting a few hours per week to building the business.

It's easy to turn satisfied retail customers into "smart consumers" who are signing up and buying at wholesale. You just let them know how to get it wholesale. What's more, it's also pretty easy to turn smart consumers— with whom you keep sharing your growing success, and who probably know a few other people who want products or are interested in the business opportunity as well— into Network Marketers. And once you do that, remember—it only takes two to five serious people to turn you into a pretty rich character.

Which brings us to "Way To Earn Money #3."

Helping People Understand What Network Marketing's All About

Well, here we are full circle—back to *understanding*. That's the third way to earn money in this business. And it's the biggest and best way of all.

Network Marketing is about building a successful team of people—a Network. No Network-building, no real success.

Retailing and referral marketing can both be profitable, but they are not what this business is about.

Network-building is.

Network-building is where the action is.

So, how do you do that? The answer is actually very simple. You find the right people and make them the right offer. Like the Godfather said, ". . . an offer they can't refuse." Only in this case, the reason they "can't refuse" is that *it's the right offer for them!* Saying the right things to the right people is what successful Network Marketing is all about.

Here's what my friend, John Fogg, wrote about that:

Give Them a Choice

Network Marketing is simply a matter
of saying the right things to the right people.

What are the right things to say?
Questions that reveal people's values, goals
and desires ...
Answers that show them how they can get what they
want through Network Marketing.

Who are the right people?
People who—once they see and hear
what you show and tell them—will
do something about it.

Your job is to give them a choice.

And here's another great piece along the same lines,
which I saw on a Networking friend's wall:

Your job is not to convince people
that this is a great opportunity,
but rather to find those people who
are searching for this opportunity
and who, upon finding it,
will do something about it.

"*Saying the right things to the right people ... Give them*
a choice ... Not to convince people, but to find people who
will do something about it ..." You see how different this
is from being a "retail-based" business, or from the high-
pressure deal of trying to "convince" lots and lots of people?

Find those people who see the big picture, people who
want to take control of their life and work—as Don Failla
says, people who want "to own their own life." That's what
Network Marketing is.

Tennis, Anyone?

Finding the "right people" is such an important concept, but a lot of people don't get it. They think that the name of the game is to enroll everyone under the sun, if possible.

And sure, talking to everyone under the sun is a great idea, and even retailing your products to the aforementioned everyone ... but remember, you're going to be working closely with the people you sponsor who are really serious about it.

Treat your Networking and team-building like a game of tennis—especially with new people. What I mean is: You've made the first move—the serve; now it's their turn. Every time they hit the ball back, you do likewise. Literally—put the ball back in their court.

This automatically empowers them to be responsible for their actions, and it makes sure you spend your time with active players. Don't hit the ball over the net twice in a row without the other person hitting it back! That's just the way the game is played.

In Network Marketing, Who Works For Whom?

In the world of conventional business, it's us and them. There's the boss and the rest of us coconuts. The boss has things he or she needs to get done (usually for his or her boss so all the bosses can keep their jobs)—and the coconuts do the doing. Since lots of work needs to get done, we've got a whole bunch of bosses and an even bigger bunch of coconuts.

If I were to illustrate this in a diagram it would look like this:

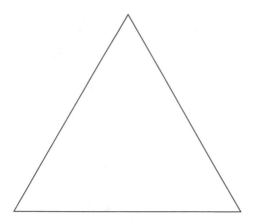

You've got it! It's a pyramid.

It's a pyramid with all the little people at the bottom doing all the hard work, while the bosses at the top tell them what to do and, by virtue of that, get to the top ranks and earn all the money. In conventional business, *you* work *for the boss.*

How is Network Marketing different?

First, no boss.

Well, that's not completely true. *You are the boss.* You're an independent contractor who works *for you.*

And that's not entirely true, either—in fact, you work "for" lots of other bosses, whom you get to choose.

You see, the real boss in Network Marketing, the person *you* work for—*persons,* actually, because there are lots of them—are all the people in your downline organization.

You work for your Network.

Now, please don't get all crazy at the thought of eventually having a Network of 500 or 10,000 bosses. Remember, I said there will be *two to five key leaders* on your first level. *Those* are the people you really work *for* directly. The other bosses you have are their downline leaders.

I consider that I work for every single man or woman who is actively building his or her business in my Network.

My job is to do everything in my power to have them create success in this business. I call that "everything in my power" "T.E.E.'ing Off—Time Energy and Effort." And what's most important to understand here is that Time, Energy and Effort are both what you are looking for *from* the people you bring into your Network, and also what you're *giving* them when you "go to work for them."

Time, Energy and Effort— T. E. E.'ing Off for Success

The first thing you want from other people is their *Time*. Success in Network Marketing requires Time—Time is the legal tender of our business.

There are two ways you get a person's Time. The first has to do with your product.

A Product Worth the Time

First, they have to understand and appreciate the value of the product. They have to like the product enough to be able to share it with people. The more they like it, the more enthusiastically they will *make the time* to offer it. (*Loving* it is even better!)

A superior product that no one wants is worth less— if not *worthless*.

There is no substitute for a superior, high-value product that outperforms the claims made for it and makes life better for the person using it. That's the kind of product you want. That's the kind of product that people will *commit their time* to trying, using and recommending.

With a product line like that, an aspiring Network Marketer is unstoppable.

The second essential element you need to offer people for their time is *the promise*.

A Promise Worth the Time

No matter what company you're with, no matter what

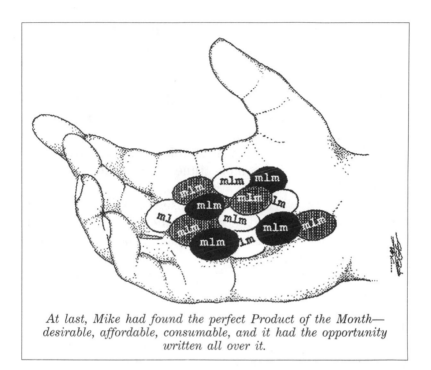

*At last, Mike had found the perfect Product of the Month—
desirable, affordable, consumable, and it had the opportunity
written all over it.*

product or service you offer, all of us in this business share
one common product—Network Marketing itself.

The promise of Network Marketing is the promise of
creating the lifestyle of which you've always dreamed. In
truth, Network Marketing is "The New American Dream."

Do something for me—better yet, *for yourself*—right
now. Take out a piece of paper and across the top write
"My Ideal Day."

Now, clear out any limitations about what you think is
possible—let's just say "anything goes." Write down what
your absolutely ideal day would be like.

Describe, in detail, when and how you wake up ... what
you do next ... your work ... your play ... how you are
with your family and friends ... Write it all down.

Does that day of yours look like the life of a millionaire?
It probably does. Would you like to know a secret? *Few*

millionaires—if any—have a day like that. They're too busy protecting the millions they've got, and making sure they earn more.

But in Network Marketing, you *can* live the "life of a millionaire"—and you can do it with significantly less income than those millionaires have. I know people earning $50,000 a year *part time* in Network Marketing—who are living literally better than most millionaires. They worry less, enjoy more, have more time to call their own and spend their time the way they want to.

Plus, they're working for themselves and never, ever have to "sell out" for the sake of money. Imagine what their lives would be like with $100,000! Imagine what your life would be like.

Now that you've got your people's Time, you also need their Effort and Energy.

Effort

Effort comes from investing your *Time*. You don't need to invest a lot of "capital," as in monetary capital—but you do need to invest your *Time*. It means work. Not necessarily hard work . . . *smart* work. And that means making the Effort to give yourself the best *education and training*.

There's a wonderful thing about learning—it is both irresistible and contagious. You simply can't keep it to yourself!

Effort also means "Paying The Price." You pay the price by setting aside an hour or two a day, or 10 hours each week to spend on your business. It may mean a night or two away from your family, friends or the things you do for pleasure. It may even mean the sacrifice of money you had planned to invest somewhere else.

Without the promise of Network Marketing (plus the promise of your own particular company and products), you won't put forth the *Effort*—and neither will the people you want in your business.

Paying the price with your *Time* and *Effort* is required for success in Network Marketing. And what they both require is your *Energy*.

Energy

The dictionary says that energy is "vigor or power in action; vitality and intensity of expression; the capacity for action or accomplishment; the ability to do work ..."

So what's the source of this energy?

To me, it's your *spirit*. Energy and spirit are synonymous. And spirit comes from God (whatever that means to you).

It's always been interesting to me that the word "enthusiasm" comes from two Greek words: *enthos*, meaning "within," and *theos*, meaning "God." So when someone is enthusiastic, they're showing you their *God within*. That says something about the power of a person's energy!

There is certainly spirit and *energy* involved in the pursuit of your goals. However, if you want to tap into the greatest resource of *energy* possible, then the key is to tap into *the greatest goal possible*.

And that goal will always have to do with being of service to others.

Real, unobstructed and unlimited, pure and powerful *energy* comes from your commitment to serve others. And what better way to serve them than to dedicate yourself to their freedom, creativity, personal and professional growth and development—in short, to their success?

And, what better vehicle to express that commitment, and to make it real through action, than Network Marketing? There simply is none.

Your First Step

If you want people's Time, Effort and Energy, you must help them create results almost immediately. If you can see that they're willing to devote the *Time* and put forth

111

Effort, it's up to you to direct that *Time* and *Effort* to produce results for them. And doing it in a timely manner ices the cake.

Wanting to get rich in this business is an okay goal. Wanting to *make others rich*—in all the ways that "rich" truly means in life—is a far greater and more powerful goal. It's a goal that empowers people to great accomplishments.

And what do you think that does for you?

Empowering people is the key. That's why I say you're working *for them*. The more successful the men and women in your Network are, the more successful *you are!*

Now, let's make a jump here to one of the most important ways you'll need to empower your people: helping them learn *how to handle objections*.

Understanding Objections— Listening to People

Most people don't really listen to others. They're too busy thinking of how to respond, what to say that will get the other person to see it their way.

If I ask you to put your hand up in front of your face, and I push against it, you're going to push back. That's what conversation feels like for most people. And that kind of "pushy" conversation is what gives rise to most "objections" people encounter in this business.

Remember I said that this business was about saying the right things? Well, you can bet if you're sitting there while the other person's talking to you, and you're thinking about what you're going to say back when it's your turn—*that's* the *wrong* thing to say!

The key to saying the right things is saying the right things *FOR THEM*. That requires listening. And when you truly listen to other people, 95 percent of all so-called "objections" disappear!

Maybe you've heard this great saying:

People don't care how much you know, until they know how much you care."

True enough. When people *feel* you empathizing with them—and that's how it comes across to them, they *feel* it because you're listening intently—they open up immediately to what you have to say.

Remember that quote about giving people a choice? Well, when you care and you listen, then people are free to choose. That's when you find out if they're the "right people" or not. Just give people an educated choice. Let them do the "work" of *making* that choice—not you.

Now, there are three basic objections that seem to come up most often in this business. Here's the first:

"Is This One of Those Pyramid Things? . . ."

Now, what are they really asking? Yes, they want to know if your company and opportunity is legal. (Well, is it?) But what they *really* want to know may be something like this:

"Are you going to make money off of me?"

Here's what I do with that; I ask them:

"Bob, if all throughout grade school, high school and college, each of your teachers and professors were going to get a percentage of all the money you earned throughout your lifetime because of what they taught you, do you think you would have gotten a better and more useful education?"

I tell them that the *only way* I earn money in this business is by helping them be successful.

Anybody got a problem with that?

End of objection #1. *Next!*

"I Don't Have the Time to Get Involved . . ."

Great! Time is exactly what I want to show them how to have *more* of!

Before I got into Network Marketing, I didn't have any time, either! The truth is, though I didn't realize it at the time, time was what I wanted most, more than money, more than any other measure of success: time with my family . . . time to play basketball . . . time to travel and be with my friends . . .

I *really* understand when people say they don't have the time. And that's exactly what I'm offering. You know what the money I earn in Network Marketing buys me most? Time—and quality time at that. That's precisely what this business is so good for—for more time!

That's the real common denominator in this business— time, especially other people's time. And for you, and for everybody to whom you show the business, other people's time is what translates directly into profit dollars.

Let people know how to work smart, by working with and through others—that they can create more time in their lives. Give them J. Paul Getty's wonderful quote, "I'd rather have one percent of 100 people's efforts than 100 percent of my own." Tell them about leverage. They'll probably know how it works with dollars, in real estate or banking, but they may not know how to make it work for them by leveraging their time, energy and effort through other people. Let them know about how it's possible to do that through Networking.

If they really don't have the time they want—then they've got to take a look at what you're showing them! *Next!*

"I Don't Have Enough Money to Get Involved . . ."

Sometimes, since they're already talking about money, they'll add:

". . . And why are these products so expensive?"

The ". . . don't have enough money" number gets a pretty straightforward reply from me.

"It hardly takes any money to begin. What's a kit and two or three products cost? Not much."

Honestly, I've known some *very* successful Network Marketers who entered the business with $100 *borrowed* from a friend.

Please—don't try to save all the broke people of the world with Network Marketing. I've found that many people who are flat broke are flat broke for a reason. If you encounter a person whose circumstances are just "broken" for the moment, you'll see the spark in them. What makes them different from other "brokes" is that if they've got nothing, they'll *go get* the small amount of money it takes to begin—no matter what it takes.

And please don't go fronting products all over the place, trying to help people who really don't want to be helped. That's a great way to lose thousands of dollars of your hard-earned money with no results but heart- and wallet-ache.

You see, "I don't have enough money to begin" is an absurd contradiction of terms in Network Marketing. That's one of the real beauties about this business—you don't *need* that kind of money!

Where else but in Network Marketing can the average man or woman invest a few hundred dollars—with the very real potential of earning as much as the CEO of a successful corporation?

The average franchise costs $85,000 just for the fee alone!

What's a small business cost to start up? You simply can't get into your own business for less than the start-up costs involved in Network Marketing.

But what if, after hearing all that, the person is still complaining about not having the money? Then you're not talking to the right person.

Move on.

About the "expensive products": Focus on the *value* of the products. Value comes from benefits and results received.

Try it. It's guaranteed. If you don't get full value from the products, give them back in 29 days and you'll get a full refund.

It's as simple as that.

IF you are a product of your product, IF you are genuinely enthusiastic and can show and tell people—using yourself as an example—just how great those products are, then they *will* see the value. And take a close look at those two "if's." Make sure that for you, they're not just if's, but sure things!

After all, if you weigh 600 pounds and are turning them onto a diet product, you'll have to expect people to be turned *off*. If you look like you haunt houses on weekends, don't expect people to see value in a nutritional product that you claim has changed your life (unless their goal is to go haunting with you).

Also, let them know that most Network Marketing products are specialty items not found in stores. Their higher quality is reflected in a higher price. Without person-to-person education about the product—which you'll almost never get in a retail store today—people won't understand the higher value of the product and it won't sell. That's one major reason the company chose to go through Network Marketing in the first place.

Are some Networked products too expensive—not worth the money—not a good value? Yes. If you've got one, go find another opportunity, because there's no way to make up for poor quality or low or no value.

So, assuming you've got the right product, with the right value, and you are a product of your product—don't let the "expensive" objection put you on the defensive. Just as some people are broke for a good reason, some people have a poverty consciousness about spending more money for greater value. That's why there are Rolexes and Timexes. That's hard to change, especially in the short time you have to be with each person.

One way I deal with that is to focus on the value of my products, and ask people: If you appreciate the higher quality and greater value, would you be interested in learning how you could easily have these products literally pay for themselves?

And the way to do that, of course, is by becoming a "smart consumer"—signing up as a distributor and purchasing at wholesale—and then spreading the good word to family and friends.

Again, I'm just looking for the right people.

"I've Tried This Before . . ."

Another objection people sometimes encounter is the "I've been involved in Network Marketing before and I didn't have a good time and I'm actually burned out on the idea and would you please go away now . . ." objection. It's a tough one, especially for beginners. Here's what I do with it.

First, I ask them to tell me the things they learned with their past experience. That's got to be first—there's no way I can understand their "objection" if I don't first get the chance to listen to them talk about it.

Now, lots of the talk you'll hear will be negative at first. But if you stick with it, probe deeper and ask them to say more about this point or that, pretty soon you'll find they're in a place where you can begin to point out how much they've actually learned. Once you do that, you can show them what a great position they're in to do it right this time. All they need, you can explain, is the right vehicle, the right company to make it work.

"The system is the solution," said an old AT&T ad, and it sure is true in this business. Make sure you show people with the "I tried before and it didn't work" objection how your company—and *your* system—are different.

By the way, when people have quit before, it's usually because that other company or their past sponsor was weak. In this case, just show them how you and yours are different, how this time, there's real staying power, personal attention and support from you, and you've got them.

A great approach is, "If I could show you a way ..." then complete the sentence with how you'll put in what was missing for them in their previous Networking encounter, ending up with "... would you be willing to take a look at my opportunity?"

If the answer is "Yes," go for it.

If the answer is "No," thank them for their time, and ask them if it's alright if you contact them again some time, just in case they change their mind.

Either way, you've done your best—and it's on to the next action step.

"How Is It Working For You? ..."

One question that sometimes turns into a stumbling block for new distributors is, "How successful are you in the business?" An all-too-common response is to turn red, then pale ... gasp for breath, croak out that your first check was $12.38—and then head for the door. Not necessary.

Try this:

*"Person's Name, I just started in this business. My
sponsor, His or Her Name, is training me and last
month, he/she made $ _____ . He/she has shown
dozens of people how to earn the money they've always wanted, and I'm going to be the next one. I
want you to do it with me."*

If your sponsor is also quite new, just keep going upline
till you find a *very* successful Networker you can point to
as an example, including how he or she is working with
you, teaching you to be successful as well.

Remember how I said that *you* is what you're really
"selling"? Well, "you" includes your sponsor and upline,
too! They're part of the package that you represent—and
don't be shy about saying so.

The Right Stuff

In Network Marketing, you are not out to bake your cakes
from scratch. You're not out there *convincing* people, or
creating interest and enthusiasm where no possibility
exists. Life is hard enough without adding *those* uphill
battles and burdens to your "things to do" list.

That's why we call this the "sorting" business. You plant
seeds, see if they sprout, sort them out, and move down
the highway of success with those folks who want to play
with you.

Remember, you only need four or five men and/or women
who want to build a business with you to succeed. So, sort
through all the people you know and meet to find the ones
who want to come to the party, earn money and have a
good time.

The right people don't have any specific background.
Age, sex, race, color, religion, education, experience, family or business background matters not at all in Network
Marketing. All you're looking for is someone who is looking for you, too.

You're looking for people who have the desire to own their own lives.

You're looking for people who want to build a business just as you're doing.

You're looking for the right people.

As long as someone has the desire—he or she is the "right people."

"You mean, all they need is desire?"

Yes.

"Do all the people who have desire succeed?"

No. These days, most people's success in Network Marketing depends on how they get started. And that's what's next, *Getting Started.*

CHAPTER EIGHT

Getting Started

GETTING IMMEDIATE RESULTS IS VITAL IN OUR BUSINESS, as I mentioned before. How long can you or your people continue to devote the time, energy and effort required to do this business without seeing real and tangible results? The answer is, not very long at all.

Jim Rohn asks the question, "How long would you want your child to be in first grade?" Same question applies in our business. One big key to success in Network Marketing is setting it up so people get immediate results.

As Dave Klaybor, president and founder of Powerline Systems, says:

> *"First, you want to become a good student, then a great student. Next, become a good teacher—and then a great teacher."*

The first step to creating fast results is learning how to talk to people when you first begin—and, maybe even more important, *which people* to talk to.

There are basically four categories of people you can talk to about your business:

1) *People You Know who ALREADY have a perception about Network Marketing;*

2) *People You Know who DON'T have a perception about Network Marketing;*

3) *People You DON'T Know who ALREADY have a perception about Network Marketing;*

4) *People You DON'T Know who DON'T have a perception about Network Marketing;*

Now, sooner or later, you'll probably talk with people in all four categories, and we'll take a look at how to approach each. But for now, ask yourself this one: When you first start doing the business, do you want to start with your friends—or with people you don't know?

"Who Ya Gonna Call?"

A lot of people, for whatever reason, don't want to approach their friends at first—it's "too risky." I use the image of a gold mine to help put this in perspective.

Let's say you've just stumbled onto a gold mine—I'm talking about a real one, with *millions* worth of honest-to-goodness gold nuggets, right in your back yard. Now, there's more gold in here than you could ever mine—let alone ever spend—in a dozen lifetimes. Obviously, there's enough to go around—way around! So . . .

. . . With whom do you want to share it?

With people who are your friends—or people you don't know?

Now, if you *really know* the mine is *that* rich, you probably want your family and friends to have first crack at sharing the wealth. Seems only natural. But if you're not sure whether that's really gold in them thar hills . . . if you have your doubts about how rich it really is, you might want to try sharing it with people you don't know first—just so it can prove itself *before* you "risk" turning your friends on to it.

I mean, you wouldn't want to get your friends' hopes up, right? Besides, you don't want to risk looking foolish to them.

Lookin' Good

It's a fact of human nature: We absolutely *HATE* to look bad in other people's eyes. Especially those people whose opinions we value most highly. And naturally, most of us place a higher value on the opinions of our family and close friends than we do on those of strangers we may never see again.

You see, we know that our friends carry a picture of us—warts and all—in the wallets of their minds. That picture is like the one in the book, *The Picture of Dorian Grey*. It just gets older and uglier! And it's covered with all your goof-ups, all the silly things you've done, all your shortcomings and weaknesses. You know that it's really hard for them to see you as a successful business person with all of that going on.

So, what do you do? Remember this one: "Let the tools do their work"—and you just be responsible for doing *yours*.

So, what's the tools' work? *Their* work is to *look good*—to be the "experts," to make a fantastic impression and provide all the information you need to provide. *Your* work is just to be the friend who shows them the tools—your work is to create the relationship.

Again, use your upline and the tools. A great, professional video will do wonders for how people see or think of you. A three-way call with your dynamic, caring sponsor can do even more. Especially, if he or she says something about how committed he or she is to changing your pattern of success for the better. That's powerful!

So don't worry about the Dorian Grey picture. Your successful Network Marketing career will change the way it looks.

Give Your Friends a Break Today

When new distributors don't approach people they already know with their Networking opportunity, I say it's because they don't believe it's a gold mine. They're playing it safe by talking to strangers first. If a few dozen strangers sign up and start to do the business successfully right away, well then, it must be okay. Now, they'll turn their friends on.

I say, approaching it that way is doing your friends a disservice.

Here's a fascinating bit of revealing statistic from James Tolleson:

Your own income equals the average of the earnings of your ten closest and best friends.

How about that! Knowing that, you now can increase your income, either by getting new friends—or, by helping all your current closest friends earn more money! And isn't that a great idea anyway!

If you're convinced that this business of ours—this business of *yours*—really can lead to a new and better lifestyle, give the people you know, like and love first shot at it.

Again, let the tools do the work. Your job here is to set it up in such a way that your friends will take a look at the tools you send them or give them. That's all you have to do.

From then on, it's a sorting process. If they get the big picture of what Network Marketing offers, they'll want to know more. If not, as John Kalench says, "SW, SW, SW—N!" Some Will, Some Won't. So What? *Next!*

I add a twist of my own to this saying of John's. Instead of *N* for *Next*, I say "N.N." for *Not Now*. For me, a person is only saying "No" for now—that's all it is, *for now*. Check back with them next week, next month, in three months. Everything in our world is constantly changing, even people's opinions and perceptions of your business opportunity. It's part of Butwin's Law:

Never Close the Door!

The Goal: Just Have Them Take a Look

There's an old salesman's adage (and since I'm an old salesman, I use it) that goes: "20—12—2." Out of 20 sales calls, you'll get about 12 appointments (people taking a look), and the average is two sales. The more people you talk to, the more who'll take a look, and the more who'll get involved.

If you were to call up strangers from your local telephone book and ask them to take a look at your opportunity, how many would do that?

If you were to call up family and friends and ask them to take a look at your opportunity, how many would do that?

For immediate results, first contact people you already know—just for a look.

The way I've found to approach these people most effectively goes something like this:

"Jim, you know I've recently been looking at alternative ways to improve my lifestyle. I want to have a more powerful life: more freedom, more time to do what I want, and more money, too. From all the research I've done, I feel Network Marketing is the best opportunity for me.

"And you know what, Jim? The biggest problem I've found in getting started in this business is other people's perceptions. Everybody seems to have a strong opinion about what this business is really about. I've seen how it has a lot of merit for myself.

And I think it can be powerful for you, too. Would you be willing to check out some information about Network Marketing if I sent it to you?"

One approach many people have used successfully with family and friends is the "What do you think of this?" approach.

People love being experts. So, leverage that.

"Hey, Mary. I just started a new business. I'm really excited about this. It's the opportunity I've been searching for. I value your opinion. I don't know if it's right for you, but I sure want to know what you think about it. Would you be willing to review the material (video, brochures, tapes, samples, whatever) about my company and product and tell me how you feel about it all?"

All I want—and all I recommend for you to want in the beginning—is to have people agree to TAKE A LOOK. That's your only job.

Your job is not to "get them into the business." That's *THEIR* job! Yours is to have them take a look.

Once they do, then the attractiveness of your opportunity, the value of your products, your enthusiasm, and their ability to see themselves creating the lifestyle they want through your opportunity—all that takes over. You can help that process along by letting them have the best tools and sharing your own excitement and passion, but it's *their* choice.

Positioning

Here's another reason why it makes sense to approach the People You Know first: *Positioning*.

Remember what I said about how putting your focus on making retail sales can give people the message that this is a "sales business"? Well, when you contact people you already know, you give *that* message, too—in other words, the message that "The way you do this business is to talk with your friends."

When you contact strangers, you give *that* message: "This is a contacting-strangers business." How many people do you know who'd jump at the opportunity to have a business where they talked—what sales pros term "cold-calling"—to strangers every day?

Right, not very many.

It's fine if *you* can do that—and in a little while here, we'll talk about that, too—but it's a whole lot easier, especially when you're starting out, to attract people to you and your business with the image of, "Just talk to your friends and have them take a look at it."

See what I mean?

The Friendship You Save Could Be Your Own

Friendship is precious. You don't want to do anything to risk the quality of those relationships. The key to keeping your friendships while building your Network Marketing business is this:

Remember that your opportunity is a gift you are sharing with your friends.

If that's how you think about it, and how you offer it to other people, there's little danger of breaching a friendship with anyone. If by chance you did—have a "friendly" mess on your hands, that is—I suspect there wasn't much of an honest, supportive relationship there anyway.

About a year ago, a woman named Rita Smith, wrote a nasty, anti-Network Marketing piece in the *Toronto Star* newspaper. It was titled "Beware of loved ones peddling products." I saw it and sent it to John Fogg.

In her article, the writer cried "Foul" about how

Networkers approach friends and family with their products and opportunity. I think she referred to it as "a despicable concept." Nice. Anyhow, Fogg sent her a reply. Here's part of what he wrote:

"*... If you were to open a conventional business, say a shop of some kind, wouldn't your first customers likely be friends and family? That's only natural. With the exception of some dysfunctional relationship problems, who's more supportive to your success than the people who love you? Why would it be any different in Network Marketing?*

"Do some MLM people abuse their close relationships? Of course, but that is not the fault of Network Marketing any more than the institution of marriage is to be held accountable for the heartbreak of child abuse.

"It's unfortunate that Ms. Smith has chosen such a one-sided view of Network Marketing.

"Whether you are approached by a loved one offering a great product they have thoroughly enjoyed—perhaps even one that has changed their life in some dramatic way— or, a dear friend encourages you to earn some extra income by joining him or her in a fun, easy, creative and enjoyable business adventure, please, be open to what's being offered. Profiting from our relationships—both giving and receiving—is one of the most richly rewarding and worthy of all human endeavors. To have that profit be expressed in the form of cash money as it is in Network Marketing ... well, what a nice innovation!

"Perhaps you could look at money as simply a symbol or measure of genuine value. When you do that, you might easily see that giving money to another person is an exchange of something more than dollars. You might even be able to see it as an expression of love. Looking at it that way, Rita Smith, if you were my sister, I'd do all I could to involve you in Network Marketing and make you a millionaire."

Puts a new light on Ms. Smith's "objection," doesn't it?

Why would you not want to share a way to create a better lifestyle with the people you care about most? Like the letter said, "it's only natural."

Now, pestering them to death—that's another matter. Remember, your job is to give people a choice—not to convince or "get them" to do anything. Network Marketing is for consenting adults *only*.

"Thou shalt not manipulate" is a great Eleventh Commandment to remember and follow, always! Influence—absolutely, but don't try to convince anybody to get involved in something they don't want to do.

If You're Going to be Santa Claus, Guess What You Need

Hint: It's something you'll be checking twice—and twice again, and twice again.

When you start your own conventional business, you need to invest substantial money in your capital assets—equipment, inventory, a plant or retail location, and the like.

In Network Marketing, there's only one capital asset, one piece of "equipment" that you need. It costs you nothing—and a good one is worth its weight in gold.

It's your Contact List.

A good Network Marketer will keep that initial Contact List—and keep developing it—for years, treating it like it was made of silk, or platinum. On the other hand, one way to tell for sure that someone in your Network is not yet really serious about building a business is when he or she procrastinates endlessly about creating that Contact List.

It really is this simple: No list, no business!

Whose names go on the list?

Depending on what particular company you're affiliated with, you may be supplied with a dynamite system for creating your initial Contact List. (It might be called your

"Prospect List," "Names List," "Sphere of Influence"—different names, but the principle is universal.) In some cases, your own upline organization might also have a terrific system to use.

In case you're on your own here, let me give you a simple, powerful, Street Smart system for making your first Contact List.

Take a piece of blank, lined paper. At the top, write "A) Friends." Below that, write the names of five friends, one line to each name. Add their addresses and phone numbers, if they're handy; otherwise, add them later, after you've finished the list.

Skip a line.

Next, write "B) Relatives." Follow that with five names. Then skip another line.

Keep going, filling in five names for each of the following categories:

C) School
D) Organizations / clubs
E) Professionals (accountants, lawyers, doctors, etc.)
F) Neighbors
G) Co-workers
H) Religious affiliations

Remember, you can add names from the past as well as those with whom you're currently in touch.

Now you'll add one last category:

I) "Never-ever People": Five people you skipped when doing A – H, because you figured, ". . . they will *never ever* be interested in this business." Trust me on this one: Experience shows that this may be the most important category!

Now you've got 45 names. Go back over the list and

read the categories again—and add another five names anywhere, making it 50.

Most of the experts say you need 100 names for a serious Contact List. This system will give you 50 in under 15 minutes—and you're halfway there. And as you progress in your business-building, you'll continue to add new names.

How to Set an Appointment

Again, your own upline or company training may have a great system for you to use for contacting these people. The important thing is that your approach is short, sweet—and especially, SIMPLE. It's got to be simple for three (very simple!) reasons:

• *You've got to know what you're going to do.* This is no time to be swimming around in a sea of choices about what to say next. Get a formula and stick to it.

• *Simple sells; Complicated confounds and confuses.* If it's complicated, elaborate, overly long or too information-heavy, it feels awkward to you and to them; your Contact is likely to be put off. A two- or three-minute attention span is not an imposing request for most people; a 20-minute audience is.

• *It's got to be a doable model.* If it's not short, sweet and simple, nobody else is going to be interested in duplicating what you're doing. Remember positioning? Enough said.

Here's an example of a short, sweet, simple and Street Smart script:

> *"John—If the right thing came along and you felt it was the right thing for you, would you be interested in improving your income? [Wait for answer] Of course, it might not be right for you [now they're*

interested!]—but if you see this the way I saw it, I think you'll be just as excited as I was. That's why I would like to share some information with you on how to develop multiple income strategies . . ."

Which you conclude with your offer and request, whatever it may be—

"I'm dropping off / sending this audio tape—when's the best time to call you later this week to see what you think of it?"

or

"I'd like to come by your office / come by your home / meet you at Gino's for lunch, etc. later this week— which is better, Thursday or Friday?"

But What If They Say "No"?

Here's how I handle that: They say:

"Robert, thanks for sending me the information (tape, samples, whatever), but I'm not interested."

I say:

"Frank, you're welcome. I appreciate your taking your valuable time to look at it. One key to my business is referrals. Is there anyone you know, somebody who's ambitious, wants a little extra income, or maybe is in a dead-end job, who'd be interested in taking a look at my business?"

Now, let's play psychology for just a minute.
This person—probably a friend of yours—has just said

"no" to you. Nobody likes to disappoint people, especially a friend. You just gave them an opportunity to make it all better. Nine times out of ten, they'll jump at the chance to help out with a couple of names. That takes the heat off them and enables them to support you, too. Win-win.

Now, I add some spice to the game:

"Frank, Network Marketing is about rewarding people fairly for their efforts. If you give me the name of someone who joins me in the business, I'll treat you with a gift certificate for dinner at Giorgio's restaurant."

That costs me $50 *only when* the referral comes into the business. But it allows me to make a juicy offer to Frank right now—and, I'm going beyond my normal Network of acquaintances, which is a major plus.

By the way, through this whole process, do you think Frank may be taking another look at how this business actually works? Maybe even thinking about how simple it is—even fun? Not all the "Franks" you talk to are doing that, but you'd be surprised how many are.

Remember Butwin's Law: Never close the door. Frank said "no," then he gave me a couple of referrals. Great. Then I ask:

"Frank, I've learned that people's circumstances change. Is it okay if I keep in touch with you? You know, send you some additional information of interest [and what I mean by this is copies of articles, newsletter reprints, anything you come across about Network Marketing] and let you know how my business is going?"

Most people say "yes," and now you've got a chance to keep your success in front of them. It's amazing how people who weren't interested in April, get *very* interested in

October when they see how you've gone from zero $$$ to a couple of thousand dollars income or more in such a short time. Just drop them a short note attached to an article or flyer saying how happy and successful you are, and how much fun you're having . . . and that's all it takes.

Success is a *very* contagious condition.

All of this is an example of the **WITHEM** principle.

WITHEM

"WITHEM" simply means: "What's In It For Them?" Everything you do with people in this business must include a clear WITHEM.

I've used the expression, "Let the tools do the work," a number of times—but it's also critical to understand what *your* work is. *Your* work is to establish the relationship and the context within which the tools will do *their* work. To prepare the way for the right tool. And that's all about WITHEM.

> *"Mary, can you see what's in this for you?"* . . . *"Sam, what was that person's WITHEM?"*

Whatever the situation—whether you're talking with a prospect in a presentation, or you're following-up with training a new distributor, looking together to see how they could refine their approach and achieve a higher percentage of success bringing people into the business— focus on WITHEM and you'll be that much closer to the truth. And in Network Marketing, the truth does set you financially free!

What makes all of this easy for me is that I'm looking for lifers—people who are committed to achieving a better life for the rest of their lives. As Robert Natiuk taught me in the beginning, I'm looking for people in whose lives I can make a difference.

Like the Zen archer going out to hunt carrying only one

arrow, I'm a sharpshooter when it comes to prospecting people into my business. I'm looking for the right people, people with the "right stuff"—people with the earnest desire to change the quality of their lifestyles to something much better.

And when I find them, I'm going to say the right things— and I'm going to let proven, results-getting tools do most of my talking for me.

My job is to interest people enough to take a look, then to help the person see and hear his or her WITHEM, and then to connect that WITHEM to my opportunity so that person *believes* he or she can do it, too!

Yes, it really is *that* simple.

Easy? Sometimes, but not always.

Simple? Always—but *always!*

Changing Perceptions

You might be surprised to realize how many people have been approached by someone in Network Marketing at some time or another—and many more know somebody else who's been approached. In fact, you might be surprised to discover just how many people have already formed some sort of opinion about Network Marketing, however vague or indirect it might be.

Job One is to reveal what that perception is—and this is true whether you're talking to family or strangers. Job Two, in most cases, is to set that *misperception* straight.

I've learned that once a person has established a perception, *your message* doesn't stand a chance of getting through unless and until you can change that perception.

Again, use the tools. There are a number of fine books and tapes that give people a great look at what this industry is truly about—and more, what the possibilities are *for them*. Use them. Let the tools do their work, especially when it comes to changing perceptions.

I covered a few of those perception changes earlier when

I spoke about dealing with "objections": the Pyramid—or, "Are you going to make money *off me* . . . ?" "I don't have time . . ." and "I don't have the money." All three of those are simply perceptions people have formed, and that you can help them change.

Another major perception people have is "sales," and we've covered that one as well. You see, perceptions are thoughts people have; thoughts are created and live in the mind. And, people change their minds all the time. So, just as when you dealt with changing your own habits of belief (habitudes), that's how you can change other people's perceptions, too—not by pushing against their hand, but by listening, understanding their perception, and helping them see "through it" to the other side.

A classic perception-changing technique that many, many Street Smart Networkers employ is the "Feel, Felt and Found" approach. It's valuable because in one short, spoken paragraph, it enables you to let the person know that you understand what his or her real concern is, that you empathize with the person because you felt the same way once, and that now, you've changed your mind on the subject (and so can they). Here's how it goes.

> *"Chris, I can appreciate just how you FEEL. When I first heard the possibilities about the kind of income you could earn in Network Marketing, I FELT they were pie-in-the-sky: $10,000 a month . . . after only a year . . . and working just part-time! That's crazy! But you know what I FOUND out? It's true. I did it, and there's no reason you can't, too. (OR) It's true. My sponsor's done it, and he's helping me to do it, too!"*

The key to changing people's perceptions is:

1) LISTEN—and let them know that you understand what they're saying and you know how they feel.

2) SHARE your own similar perceptions—thoughts and feelings. And;

3) SHOW them the other side of it—tell them what changed your mind.

One, two, three—it's that easy.

I know people want this business to be real hard. I guess that way, they feel they can justify earning so much money in such a short period of time. In fact, I felt that way in the beginning. But I found Network Marketing was actually easy. And once I understood that, I started earning big money and having even bigger fun.

See what I mean? Feel, Felt and Found. It's easy.

When you understand people's resistance, and you learn how to dissolve that with empathy, bingo, you're on your way to the top. People may hate to be sold, but they love to buy—and somebody's gotta do it!

So, talking with the People You Know is the way to get started with momentum. But you can't stay there forever. Once you've created a good start, it's time for . . .

. . . Talking With People You Don't Know

How do you meet people you don't know? It's impossible not to!

On planes, buses, trains, standing in lines, going out, going in, in restaurants, at sporting events, in hotel lobbies. Fact is, people you don't know are everywhere. I never experience a lack of people I don't know—except at home. So, rule number one: To meet people you don't already know, don't stay home. In other words—GET OUT OF YOUR COMFORT ZONE!

Ahhhhhha!! Scary, isn't it?

Perhaps; but once you get your feet wet talking to people you don't already know, it's the most fun you can have—

and, as a Networker, the most profitable fun for sure.

Think about this: 99 percent of all the people who are in my Network organization today were strangers to me five years ago! It's true. That's the way it is for every Network Marketer I've ever met. We have an unspoken credo in our industry:

A stranger is simply a friend you haven't met—yet.

The other day, I went to a new dentist, and he's already interested in the business!

There I am, sitting in his chair, paying him a couple of hundred bucks to work on my teeth. He owes me a listen! Really.

I've got a way for that dentist to dramatically alter the course of his life. I know how he can have the lifestyle he's always wanted. By asking him some simple questions, I found out that he's concerned about putting two daughters through college, and his lack of free time is killing him.

What do you think I spoke to him about?

That kind of behavior, the willingness to talk to "strangers" even when they are playing around with drills in my mouth, wasn't always within my comfort zone. But I quickly found out that if I was going to succeed in this business, I was going to have to start talking to people I didn't already know.

The Friends I Hadn't Met—Yet

I went through my list of "warm market" family and friends in a couple of weeks. Their referrals and their referrals and their referrals kept me going a good while longer. But eventually, I got to the end of the "I know you" list . . . and the end of my comfort zone.

So, I took a deep breath and talked to the guy next to me on the plane. He didn't get into the business—but he didn't kill me either.

No, I am not "willing to be open" to taking a look at an opportunity that would allow me to spend more time with my kids.

Then I talked to a waitress in a restaurant, asked her if she worked at any other job, started to learn a little bit about where she was at in her situation and aspirations. She didn't get in, either ... but I lived through that encounter, too.

Well, I was feeling pretty good about risking my life and living to see the next sunrise, so I kept on talking, improving my ability to ask questions and learn about people, and also improving the clarity of the message that I was sending.

You know about the learning curve, right? You get better as you go along, learning and mastering the thing you're doing. Well, that began to happen for me. And it will for you, too. Like the sneaker ad says, "Just do it."

139

So I talked to another guy on a plane, and *he was interested!* No kidding. I almost couldn't believe it. I gave him some tools to take home ... discovered his WITHEM right then and there on the plane ... called him up two days after he got back home ... and *Bingo!*—he's in.

Why? Because he was "right people," and he really got the message of how I was going to go to work *for him!* That's the key.

And you know, this talking to strangers things was getting to be fun. (There's a fun curve as well as a learning curve.) In fact, there was a point when I had so much fun stepping out of my comfort zone that I started to actually look for the most outlandish ways to talk to strangers I could find.

Street corners: "Pardon me, if I could show you a way to have all the time and financial freedom you've ever dreamed of, would you be willing to take this tape home and listen to it?" Men's rooms (haven't tried ladies' rooms— I guess that one's still out of my comfort zone) ... during basketball games (in which I was playing) ... I mean, anywhere and everywhere.

Remember, I'm standing there with this great gift in my hands and I'm going to give it to anybody who's up for taking it ... anywhere ... anytime. I've been doing this for so long now, it's second nature to me. With the exception of those "low life" places none of us wants to go to (and, yes, the ladies' room), I can't think of anywhere I wouldn't go to talk to people. My comfort zone has expanded to global proportions. And I've lost count of the men and women I first met as strangers who are now my good friends.

Common Sense

When you do take that deep breath, relax, and start talking to someone from the People You Don't Yet Know category, here's what changes the encounter from being one with a "stranger," into one with "a friend you just haven't met yet": *Common Sense.*

In the art of conversation, Common Sense means establishing interests, pursuits, hobbies, attitudes, experiences or any other points you have in common. Once you've discovered some point of commonality, you and this other person have a basis for relating, which means that they have a basis for trusting your opinion. The more points you discover in common, the greater the basis.

Once you establish a Common Sense, you are no longer strangers. And you know what? You never were! You were actually friends—who just hadn't discovered yet *why* you were friends!

Be the Messenger—Not the Message

You know what's enabled me to learn to talk to people I didn't know—and feel comfortable with it? Even, *enjoy* it? I am *NEVER EVER REJECTED.*

It's true. I make the introduction, quick and easy. If someone doesn't want to talk, that's okay. I understand.

I qualify them. I do that by asking a trail of questions that leads to whether or not they are the right people and this is the right opportunity for them—sort of like Hansel and Gretel leaving those pebbles behind so they could find their way home. Also, I know I need to determine if I want to go to work for them. So, as much as they're checking me out, I'm doing the same thing with them. Believe me, it's a great equalizer.

I check out if they'd be interested in receiving the information I want to send them—and I do that *first.* If so, it's "Read this . . . Listen to this . . ." I give them a tool. Even if they do want to talk, I give them a tool—if they will commit to listen or read it.

Then, after they've read, listened to, or seen what I give them, if they're not interested—it isn't personal to me. They just didn't get the message of the tool. They've

141

rejected the tool—not me. So, I hug the tool and help it feel better . . . and move on. SW, SW, SW—NN!

The more you do this, the more you refine your skills and the more new and wonderful stories you have to tell people. And if this business is about one thing above all else, it's about telling fun and interesting stories about great products and great people.

Folks, one thing every Street Smart Networker knows like the back of his or her own hand, is this:

Prospecting is about the message—NOT the messenger.

The message is the story. Tools give great messages. All you have to do is be the messenger.

We'll get to more specific techniques you can use to attract people you don't know to your business in a bit. For now, I just want you to get the point about getting out of your comfort zone and talking to strangers—it's fun and freedom all in one. And, it's a great way to earn money in Network Marketing. Let the tools help.

I just look for a good attitude in people. You can always tell when someone has a good attitude. Look for previous success trends in their lives. Go for happy, successful strangers, that's all. Sure, be selective. Remember, you want to go for the gold.

The Message is: "I'm Having Fun"

Now, you may be saying to yourself:

"But isn't all this talking to strangers sending THEM the wrong message about Network Marketing? I mean, HAVING to talk to strangers sends the wrong message of what this business is about—doesn't it?"

Good, Good! I know how you *feel*. I *felt* that way at first. But what I *found* . . . (Just kidding.)

No, the message that talking to strangers sends is fine—although I can see how this might seem like a contradiction. But remember, the idea was to get immediate results by talking with the People You Know—at first. Once you've gotten comfortable doing that, it's easier to get comfortable talking with strangers, and then it's easy to telegraph that message to them, too—that this is fun.

What I've found was that the message those strangers got from me was that this business is so easy and so much fun for me, that they wanted part of that for themselves, too.

The ability to talk effortlessly and effectively to strangers is something lots of people would love to do, but they don't. They're afraid. So, the possibility of easily speaking with strangers becomes just another freedom benefit which Network Marketing offers people.

Ask yourself: Would you enjoy being so confident and free that you could walk up to just about anybody, anywhere, at any time, and talk with them about what's most important to them in their lives?

It's one of the greatest freedoms in the world. And you can master it in two weeks or less. Honest.

How? Just do it . . . and let the tools do the work.

(I've put a list of the tools I've used successfully, with brief descriptions of each one and where to get them, in the back of the book; it's called "Great Tools I Have Known and Loved.")

Getting A Commitment

Now, once people express an interest in the business, I use company tools about the product, the marketing plan, etc. to have them get an understanding about the business and what we're up to. I connect their WITHEM to the opportunity and give them the choice. If they are interested in getting involved, it's commitment time.

I will not bring someone into *my business* and spend

time with them without that person making a commitment to doing *the business*. That's a rule—no exceptions!

I used to get anybody who said they'd give it a shot to sign up. WRONG. They never stick with it. No commitment—no possibility. Big waste of time. BIG! And time, my Street Smart friends, is your most valuable asset!

The person's commitment is required for me to bring someone into my business and spend the time to train and develop them. I recommend you do the same.

The commitment I'm after is that person's WITHEM plus some degree of time, energy and effort devoted to accomplishing their goals. I do this for a number of reasons which are beautifully explained in the following quote.

Until there is commitment there is hesitancy, the chance to draw back, always ineffectiveness. Concerning all acts of initiative and creation there is one elementary truth, the ignorance of which kills countless ideas and splendid plans: That the moment one definitely commits oneself, then providence moves too. All sorts of things occur to help one that would otherwise never have occurred. A whole stream of events issues from the decision, raising in one's favor all manner of unforeseen incidents and meetings and material assistance, which no man could have dreamt would have come his way. I have learned a deep respect for one of Goethe's couplets:

"Whatever you can do, or dream you can—begin it;
Boldness has genius, power and magic in it."

W.H. Murray, *The Scottish Himalayan Expedition* 1951

I want you to have an experience that really brings home what I mean by "commitment." So do this with me: Ask yourself:

*"Will my children [and if you don't have kids, use
'my spouse' or 'my parents'] ever starve to death?"*

Take this question seriously; what's your answer?

I have *never* met *anyone* who said anything other than
"No!—never; not a chance!" And they say it immediately,
apparently without any thought or hesitation at all.

Now, here's the interesting thing: The truth is, *you have
no proof for making that statement.*

The truth is, you really don't know what's going to
happen tomorrow—or two, or 200 tomorrows from now.
How could you possibly control the future? You can't. There
is absolutely no evidence whatsoever that your kids (spouse,
parents) will not starve—yet you will state with total
certainty that it will *never happen to them.*

How can you do that? You can do that because *you are
committed* to it. That's all. There is no more to say.

That is commitment at its clearest and most compelling.
It has nothing to do with *how* a thing will or will not be
accomplished. Commitment is simply, powerfully and without question, what you say *will* be done. The how of it all
doesn't matter—*at all*—to the making of the commitment
itself. Commitment has nothing to do with *how*. Commitment is what will happen—*no matter what.*

And it has nothing to do with "trying." Jedi master Yoda
said it perfectly in the Star Wars movie: "Luke, you either
do, or do not. There is no 'try'."

The Greek philosopher/mathematician Archimedes,
who'd gotten pretty fired up about discovering the principle of leverage, is supposed to have said,

"Give me a place to stand, and I can move the world."

Commitment is that place to stand.

I know that "love makes the world go 'round." I also
know that commitment makes it productive and fun. That's
why it's mandatory in my business.

Why I Offer the Opportunity

And while I'm speaking of commitment, you may be wondering, "Robert, you mean, you look for commitment right away? Or, after *they've* had a chance to get to know and become a product of your product?"

Well, you'll hear some people in this business say it's best to offer everyone the product first, and then show them the opportunity later on. That's not how I do it, or how I recommend you do it.

I take the approach of offering the business opportunity first, for two reasons.

First, that's how I get to connect with that person's WITHEM. It's how I get close to his or her dreams. Without that, all I've got is the possibility that sometime down the road, they *might* become interested in the business. What I'm after is giving the person the opportunity to create a new and better lifestyle, and that happens through the opportunity.

I'm after business-builders. So I put business-builder bait on my hook. If I were making a garden and wanted carrots, I'd plant carrot seeds—not squash seeds. So, I lead with the business opportunity, because that's the kind of person I want—someone interested in building a business that can create the lifestyle he or she has always wanted.

When you find someone who is interested in the business, it's an easy matter to then put the product line in perspective for them—to explain how the opportunity is anchored in the product line and their market demand.

The second reason I offer the business first is that if they say "no" to doing the business, I can still offer them the products either as retail customers or as smart consumers. (But if I offered the products first, and they said "No" to that offer, where could I go from there? "Next . . .")

There are only three possible answers to the question of whether the person I'm talking to wants to do the business with me:

1) Yes.
2) No—but I really like these products.
3) No—and I don't care for the products either.

The proven percentages are that between 33 and 50 percent of all the people you talk to will try the products or enter the business with you. Obviously, the smaller percentage will come into the business. Either way, those are decent odds.

The money-back guarantee enables people to try the products for a month at no risk. The placebo effect—a scientific rule discovered in blind studies of various types of drugs—says that one third of the people will have a positive response; one third will have no response or a negative one; and the final one third won't know if they did or didn't. So, 33 percent of the people who try your products with a money-back guarantee will get good results. If you can help them see the value of the products, and even go one step further and see the extra value of becoming a smart consumer, you'll have one third of the people you speak with buying your products, and you'll earn income from what they buy.

Now, the one third who *don't know* whether or not they got good results includes a fair number of people who can be persuaded to stick with it until they do. Give them more educational material about the products, share your own and other people's positive results with the products—and you'll have a number of these people decide they're positive for them.

So your odds are really pretty good for having half the people you talk to and present the products to end up happy with them and wanting to continue buying them from you. It's a numbers game—and the numbers are stacked in your favor.

New Distributor Bonding

So, once you've established the person's commitment, it's time to "bond" them to all aspects of their new opportunity. The first thing you want to do with your new distributor is bond them to the products, the company, the company's training programs—and, last but not least—to you and your upline.

Give them as much information as you can without "Data Dumping" them. You can kill people with too much information; by letting the tools do the work, you prevent that kind of mind-overload.

Support them in seeing the uniqueness of the products, how valuable they are for people, what the market potential is, and more. Really, *sell* them on all of it: the products, the people, the plan. Keep adding more fuel to their fire of enthusiasm. Build a bonfire of passion within them.

Let them know in no uncertain terms how the company and the products justify the business—that is, that the entire business structure and financial picture is grounded in the bona fide distribution of a highly valued product. That should be pretty simple—without the products there is no business!

Once you've done that with the new distributor, you want to help her be in action in building her own business.

The key to remember here is that the way *you* started with them is the way *they* will start with their prospects. And a head start in any endeavor is a big, big plus!

"We Do It All For You"—NOT!

Sometimes, being a Street Smart Networker requires what people call "tough love." And sometimes, that's hard to do.

Network Marketing is the people-people business, and because it is, it's natural for most of us to have a drive to care for others, to take care of them and make sure they're okay. It's one of the most wonderful aspects of our business; one of the things that sets us apart from other enterprises and industries—and it's also a trap.

When we see a new distributor struggling, it's only natural to want to step in and ease his or her way. They're having trouble getting past their fears and doubts, so we say, "Hey, I'll call them for you ... No problem, I'll do the interview. You just sit there and watch ... Don't worry, I'll have someone with more experience present the compensation plan ..."

In a word: WRONG! Let me tell you a story.

One day, a man found the cocoon of an Emperor moth and excitedly took it home to watch the creature emerge. Soon, a small opening appeared, and for several hours after, the moth struggled, but could not seem to fit its body past a certain point.

Deciding that something must be wrong, the man took a pair of scissors and snipped away the hindering part of the cocoon. The moth then came out easily, but its body was large and swollen, with small and shriveled wings.

The man expected that in just a few short hours, the moth's wings would unfurl in all their majestic, natural beauty—but they did not. Instead of developing into a magnificent creature, free to fly, the moth spent its existence dragging around a bloated, misshapen body with small, shriveled and completely useless wings.

It soon died, and the man mourned its fate.

What he did not realize was that he was the cause of the moth's deformity and untimely death. For the constricting cocoon and the struggle to pass through the tiny opening are nature's way of forcing vital fluids from the moth's body into its newly developing wings. The creature's struggles were required for its survival and fulfillment.

The "merciful" snip of the scissors was, in reality, the cruelest cut of all.

Here's another way of saying this that I sometimes use to get the point across:

When you joined our company, you signed an INdependent Distributor Form—not a COdependent Distributor Form!

Duplication—Go Ye Forth and Multiply

The primary reason I use tools to do the work is that they are *completely duplicatable.* Anyone can use them.

Not everyone can be an expert about the products. Not everyone can be an expert about Network Marketing, the compensation plan, prospecting, etc. But everyone can be an absolute master of using good tools.

I don't rely on tools because I'm lazy—I use the tools because they usually do a better job than I can at providing people with the right information the same way over and over again, *plus* all the people I bring into the business can use them, too. I can duplicate my successful actions easily using tools. That enables me to multiply my results with others, and it makes it easy for them to do the same thing with their people ... and theirs ... and so on.

Tools are convenient for prospects, too. They are free to look or listen to the tape or read the book or brochure, when they want, where they want. (Does that sound familiar? It should. It's the way doing this business is, too!) So, I spend less time per prospect and can contact that many more prospects in the same amount of time.

Also, remember the saying, "The right tool for the job." Like an auto mechanic, different jobs require specific tools. So do different people. Match the tool to the person's needs, circumstances and style, and that's the "right tool for the job." So, be flexible and choose your tools wisely.

Also, tools handle all the repetitive explanations, so I don't have to say the same thing over and over again. And that used to drive me crazy!

Can you see how you can build a huge Network organization of people all doing the same thing by simply letting the tools do the work?

Tools also enable people to get out of the gate going full blast. Imagine how long it would take to train new distributors to have a working knowledge of all those products, company history and mission, Network Marketing, the compensation plan, and more. Wow! Months—minimum.

Remember, I said I know people who've been in the business *for years* who don't understand it yet? Well, the tools understand *right now!* Using them allows a brand new person to hit the ground running like a successful, seasoned pro. That's just what tools are: proven professionals—your partners in profit.

Lead your people by example. Focus them on committing to and achieving their first achievement level. Your job is to help them see what's possible to attain. Don't have them go for what *you* want for them. Focus on what *they* want.

Stretch them a bit, but don't go so far beyond their abilities that they're destined to fail. Champion them. Be a coach, teacher, trainer and cheerleader for them.

Remember, everybody's different. Some people can bring in five people in 60 days. Some can do that in their first week. Explore the possibilities with them and then, together, create a plan of how the two of you are going to accomplish that.

Now, notice, I said *the two of you.* DO NOT LET NEW PEOPLE GO IT ALONE. Why? Because you want them to experience immediate success (which benefits both of you)—and because you want *them* to do the same thing you did with them with *their* people.

Duplicate and multiply.
Duplicate and multiply.
Duplicate and multiply.
Duplicate and multiply.
Duplicate and multiply.

And don't stop till you reach the top!

CHAPTER NINE
Black Belt MLM

READY? OKAY—HERE COMES AN ARSENAL OF IDEAS THAT can make a big difference in your success.

Some of these ideas are little tips and techniques I've used successfully in the past. Some are blockbuster concepts that can make all the difference in the world in the speed and power you have to succeed in this business.

What they all add up to is *Black Belt MLM*.

First is one of the blockbusters: Follow-through.

Follow-Up and Follow-Through

Let's face facts: No tool will be any good to you at all if you don't follow up and follow through with the person you gave it to. Follow-through is the single most missing element in the way people approach this business. When I work with someone who's having difficulty succeeding in this business, 99 times out of 100 the problem is improper or simply inadequate follow-up and follow-through.

I do the great majority of my follow-up over the phone. I'll explain why in a moment; first I want to give you the "lay of the land" in telephone follow-up.

When you first speak with someone, no matter what approach to that conversation you're using, your first

152

objective is to *establish rapport.*

Okay so far? Okay, now guess what your initial objective is when you call back your prospective business partner? *To RE-establish rapport.*

Before you begin, make certain this is a good time to talk. (You don't have to be psychic; just ask, "Is this a good time to talk?") If you don't do this, you can have a ten minute conversation that falls on unhappy, deaf ears— and upsets the other person to boot! It's the surest invitation to a "No" there is, so first check out if this is a good time. If it's not, arrange for another, better time.

Start with, "Hi, hello, how are you? ..." and find out how they're *really* doing. If it's someone that you haven't yet met in person, or someone you just met recently and this is your second real contact, you want to anchor them back to where you left them when you last spoke.

Now's the time to verify that they actually got the information you sent. Too often the post office does not deliver the packages you send as quickly as you expected.

Once you know that they got what you sent, and that they read, listened to, or watched it, then ask, "Well, what do you think? What's there that interests you?" And you're off and running.

Why I Use The Telephone

The reason I choose to do my follow-up over the phone is *positioning.* It's similar to the strategy of not positioning my opportunity as a selling business.

There's a book title that includes the phrase: "Your life and work become one." That's the message I want people to get from the way I do business: "Network Marketing can be done part-time, over the telephone."

In the past, Network Marketing used to involve doing three to five presentations a week, and a meeting or two. That's passé ... extinct. You need to be able to show people how this business will fit in with the normal course of their

The doctor confirmed her diagnosis: Throckmorton was suffering from Chronic Upline Sponsor's Syndrome.

lives. That's what shows them how they can have the lifestyle they're looking to achieve. People need to be able to buy into this business, so I want to make sure that what I do is extremely duplicatable—and that people can see themselves doing it.

That's one of the reasons I do what I do over the phone.

Also, the telephone is less confrontational, less threatening. Most people don't have a strong self-image; they lack self-esteem. They don't have the sales experience that I've got and they won't be ready, able or willing to do a formal presentation properly, right off the bat.

That's why I just use the tools that we've talked about. Anybody can do that. What's more, it's simple and easy to duplicate, so they can do the same thing with their people, and their people can, too, and so on.

There's another big positioning point to the tools-and-telephone approach.

Show Them A Time-Leveraging Business

How long does it take to hand somebody a book, cassette or video? Minutes, right?

Okay, how long does it take to give somebody a formal, sit-down presentation about your business, product, opportunity, etc.? 30 minutes . . . 45 minutes . . . an hour or more?

Now, how many people do you know who have that chunk of time to spare? I don't care whether you're talking to a homemaker or the CEO of a major corporation, *nobody* has that kind of spendable free time anymore. So, when you show them a business that can be done in minutes, as they walk through their normal lives, and followed up on over the phone in just minutes as well, you'll get their attention more often—and their commitment, too.

Just think about it for a moment: To which business approach would *you* be most attracted?

You want successful people in your business. Successful people are busy people. What busy, successful people don't have a lot of is *time*. If you show them a way they can have the rewards of a successful Network Marketing career with the least time commitment possible, your odds of getting them into the business shoot way up!

I structure 99 percent of my time around the phone. In fact, most everybody that I know who is making significant dollars in this business does the majority of their work on the phone.

You know the old adage, "Don't do as I DO . . . do as I SAY!" Well, it doesn't work anywhere in life—and especially not in Network Marketing! No matter what you *tell* your people, they will probably do what they see you *doing*. Leading by example is critical in this business, because your people DO duplicate your efforts. Using the phone works—and it not only works for me, but it's also the example I want to be setting for all my business-building associates.

Of course, there are times and places where face-to-face meetings are both appropriate and productive. Those meetings are best for the people in your local area or if you're traveling there for a training. But when you're actually working the business, people are most effectively in touch with you, and you with them, through the phone.

Setting Appointments or Doing The Business

Many people have been taught over and over again about using the phone *only* to set appointments. I disagree!

Because of my sales background before I got into Network Marketing, I learned a lot about leveraging my time with the telephone.

When I used to do selling, I looked at the whole conventional process: Making an appointment, which took time ... then adding maybe a half-hour drive to meet that person ... then being there face to face with him or her for about an hour ... and then taking another half-hour, more or less, to get to my next appointment—I added all that up, and found that's two hours!

In that same period of time, I could (and can) talk with six to eight people on the phone!

The difference using the phone makes in my personal productivity is amazing!

One great "telephone tool" is using the speaker-phone for local meetings. Want to have the CEO of your company or your rich and famous upline super-sponsor drop in for your meeting? Just rig up a speaker phone, synchronize your watches and have them call at the appointed time to talk with your people.

One small step for them. One big one for you and your people.

I've done this a lot with distributor groups around the

country, and it's fantastic! It works beautifully, and creates a great impression—"They actually got on the phone to speak just to US!" That does wonders for the self-esteem of the group in that living room.

What's Your Time Worth?

Another thing to know about your time is what its *value* is.

Quite often people in Network Marketing have large expectations for what they are looking to earn. So here's what you've got to do—for yourself and for others:

Value your time today in proportion to what you expect to earn down the road.

If you want to earn $5,000 per month, then your time— *today, right now!*—has got to be *worth* $5,000 per month.

You've probably heard about a $50-an-hour person doing a $10-an-hour job. If your goal is $5,000 a month, and you're willing to devote 10 hours each week to your business, your time is worth nearly $1,200 per week—or over $100 per hour. I don't know anybody driving a cab or even a limo who's making $100 per hour. That's why using the phone *efficiently* is well worth it for you.

Now, I even leverage my training by using the phone. Here's one way I do that:

I ask everybody in my Network to get an inexpensive little device from a place like Radio Shack (it goes for about $15) that lets them tape all their telephone conversations. It's a cord with a phone jack that plugs into the phone line, and another end that plugs into your tape recorder.

Now, if I'm going to spend my time teaching and training somebody, I want to make sure that person really gets the message. But the typical person is only going to retain about 25 to 30 percent of whatever we talk about. With our conversation being recorded on tape, that person knows he doesn't need to remember all that's being said. He can give his full attention to our conversation—and his full attention is exactly what I'm looking for.

And then, they can go back over that conversation by replaying the tape in the car or wherever, over and over again, whenever the time is best for them. This continually reinforces the message, is the ultimate in convenience, and allows the person to pay full attention without taking notes or trying to remember something he won't remember anyway.

Of course, you can tape all kinds of conversations—not just to hear what your sponsor is telling you, but to hear yourself, too. I really found it useful when I began prospecting and on two-way calls with my sponsor. We rarely get a chance to listen to ourselves, and by listening to my own taped conversations, I noticed things I wouldn't have been aware of any other way. I learned when I wasn't listening, what speech patterns I had that weren't effective (such as saying "ah" much too often), and lots of other helpful things.

I've even had people send me tapes of their conversations; after I listen to them (at *my* convenience), I can get back to them and help them get better at what they're doing.

Taping conversations is a powerful tool. It amazes me that more people don't do it. But you know, everybody's got to be somewhere. I'm glad that I'm next to my tape recorder and my telephone.

Partnerships For Profit

Who are the people you bring into business with you?

For me, there's only one answer to that—they're my partners.

I think if Network Marketing has taught me one thing above all else, it's the awesome power of partnership. That, more than anything else, is what our business is about:

People in partnership with each other, striving towards a common goal.

My Street Smart friends, your partners are the most powerful tools of all.

The original meaning of the word "sponsor" comes from Greek and has the same definition as Godfather or Godmother, which means someone who has the responsibility for the spiritual and financial well-being of the Godchild. In a very real sense, that's what being a sponsor in Network Marketing means.

My friend John Fogg, who sometimes tends to talk like an oriental mystic, says there is a yin and yang, a front and a back to everything, like two sides of a coin. He says that along with the "front" of tremendous freedom offered in Network Marketing comes an equal and balancing "back"—responsibility.

The way that responsibility shows up most for me is in my partnerships with the people I sponsor. My job, as I see it, is to help my partners grow into all that they want to become in this business. And that brings up a key point— growth.

The Personal Growth Business

Personal growth and development thrives in Network Marketing, and here's the reason why: We are in the "people business," so the knowledge and insight gained by and about people in our business is directly proportionate to our success. It's the people who are passionate about their own personal development and about their people's development who are most successful in Network Marketing.

In my group, books and especially tapes on personal and professional growth are always flying around from person to person. I'm constantly sending Wayne Dyer's tapes and Stephen Covey's tapes to my people. Every time I discover anything that will give people more insight into themselves or our business, I buy it and send it out.

Also, remember: The man or woman who graduates from college today and stops studying tomorrow will be uneducated the day after.

Going with the 80/20 Flow

Now, I do not have a partnership with everyone I've ever sponsored. The "Pareto Principle," also known as the "80/20 Rule," applies here: 20 percent of my people are responsible for 80 percent of my groups results—in terms of volume, dollars, recruiting, etc.—so I focus my partnershipping on that 20 percent. Leverage is law in Network Marketing, and you've got to leverage all your time, energy and effort by giving it to the people who are producing the greatest results.

So, 80 percent of my time goes to supporting my "20-percenters"—the players and performers in my organization. The other 20 percent of my time is spent in developing those people who want to break out of the 80 percent into the performer category, and to finding new partners who are destined to be 20-percenters.

When I was in sales, I learned that you never ever fight against the forces of the marketplace. That means, if you're in a traditionally slow selling period, don't throw advertising money away trying to change that. It's what a successful investor friend of mine means when he says, "I never fight the tape [the Dow Jones Average] and I never fight the Fed [the Federal Reserve bank]."

Back in the '60s, we had a similar expression that just sounded a little different: "Go with the flow."

When you focus your time and effort on your top 20 percent who are the producers and performers in your organization, you're going with the most powerful income flow you've got working for you. Those people are your partners in profit.

Partnerships Depend on Shared Commitment

There are two ingredients that are required in order to create strong partnerships: Having a commitment and a goal worth sharing.

There's that word again, "commitment." And it really is a crucial element in your success.

You don't have a partnership unless each of you knows what the other is committed to, and each of you buys into the other person's commitment. Unless the person I'm working with has a commitment to create great success in this business, I simply don't have time to work or play with them. And the bigger the commitment the better!

Have you ever heard this saying?

If your goal is to clear the fence and you aim for that ... maybe you'll make it and maybe you won't. But if you shoot for the moon, you're bound to clear the tree tops!

That's why I look for a solid commitment, and a big goal as well.

Remember earlier when I referred to goals as "Golds"? That's what they are, because they are so valuable for your success.

Mark Yarnell, one of our industry's true super-stars (Mark became a millionaire in less than four years and now earns as much as $200,000-plus a month), says the key to his success was having a goal bigger than he is. Mark is one of the biggest contributors to the United Way in America and he's built a state-of-the-art drug and alcohol treatment center in Reno, Nevada. That's having a goal bigger than he is. Mark says that since he's always working for a greater good than simply his own personal wealth, he's got even more support, even more power to accomplish his dreams. I agree.

The point here is that you and your partners need to

share each other's commitment and goals. That's what partnerships are based on. That's what gives them power to succeed.

Some Practical Partnership Examples

Three-way calling is a perfect example of partnerships in action.

I used three-way calling a tremendous amount when I was first building my business, and I still do it today—and I enthusiastically recommend it to everyone in my organization.

Three-way calling is a simple, $3- or $4-per-month investment with your local phone company that gives you the ability to conference with another person on calls. It's a perfect way to help your new people make their first calls to prospects with you on the line. They can introduce you . . . you do most of the talking . . . and they not only have a better chance at getting the results they want, but they're also trained in the process.

In terms of positioning, the message it sends to prospects is that *you don't do this business alone* . . . that the experienced sponsor is there to help. And that's a great first impression to make on new people. Right away, they get the teamwork and support that's available in this business. It's great.

By the way, if someone asks me to call someone *for* them, I refuse. But I'm always happy to do it *with* them. You either give people fish or teach them how to fish so they can feed themselves. Me, I love to fish—*and* to teach other people where all the fish are.

Another example of partnership in action is the buddy system. This is where you connect two people in your group to work together, giving each other support and assistance in their business-building efforts.

I've seen buddies who check in with each other on a daily basis, report their progress back and forth, uncover and solve problems together, etc. It's another way that partnerships make doing the business easier, and as they say, two heads are better than one.

Resources

Where do you go to look for leads and to meet new prospects?

First, look to the places you hang out, frequent and enjoy. If you're the kind who cruises art museums, look there. I got a couple of good distributors who were my basketball buddies first.

Look for groups of leaders: Churches and religious groups, civic and social clubs, Networking groups (who have mixers and breakfasts, etc.), sports clubs and gatherings, Toastmasters, Dale Carnegie, weight loss centers, spas and health clubs, your local Chamber of Commerce, business associations . . . all of these and more are excellent places to meet successful people who may be interested in the gift of your opportunity.

You can also "target market" by selecting a specific kind of person or group of people whose life circumstances fit your product or opportunity. Women with babies at home are a good example. Often you'll find they'd love to have additional income, yet most jobs require they leave their babies in the care of others. What if you could show them a better way . . . a way to have their cake and eat it, too?

You can get the names and addresses, even telephone numbers of these people, and just about any other group of people you want to reach, by talking to direct mail specialists. If you want a list of 50-year-old widowers, earning less than $32,628 per year, who live in houses which are 87 percent paid for and who play golf with a handicap of 10 or lower—it's available. Just be creative and pick whom you'd like to go after. List brokers are listed in the yellow pages; advertising agencies and newspapers can also give you their names.

Of course, one of the best and least expensive ways to attract people is to use your products in public. Sitting in a restaurant and putting a bottle of this or that on the table will inevitably bring inquiries from other customers and serving people alike. Don't be shy. Just display your wares and let human curiosity take its course.

Non-profit groups are also a rich resource of potential Network-building material. Churches, Little League and the like are always looking for ways to generate money. Could your product and your opportunity work for them? Meet with them and explore the possibilities.

Looking for a great opening line? Try this: "Has anyone ever asked you to be involved with [your company's name] company? ... No? ... I'm really surprised. You're just the kind of savvy person who'd really be great at ..." Just try that one and watch people's reactions.

"Really? Why do you say that?"

Now you've definitely got their interest!

The Power of Indexing

As important as it is to be creative in seeking out resources, it's even more important to create your own "people resource bank" by *indexing*.

What do I mean by "indexing"?

Simple: Whenever you talk with people, make notes of the most important points of interest you learn about them. And remember, "most important" means most important *to them*.

For example, birthdays (and wives' and husbands' and kids' birthdays as well as their own), other dates that are important to them, hobbies and special interests they care about, kids' athletic or artistic achievements ... whatever strikes your ear as being important to them.

And most of all, *anything* that has to do with their WITHEM—whatever represents what they're looking to achieve, earn, acquire, accomplish or attain—whatever "success" means to them.

There are three crucial elements in your successful indexing: 1) you've got to keep your ear attuned to these important personal elements; 2) you've got to develop the habit of writing them down right away, either during the conversation or just after you hang up or part company; and 3) you've got to have a well-organized, always-accessible place to write them!

Whatever form of indexing suits you is fine; the most common (and most commonly effective) are file box (for 3 x 5 cards), notebook or diary, and daily planner. Remember: The most important feature of your indexing is that you need to be able to retrieve that information in an instant the next time you talk with that person; so make sure you organize your personal indexing with a system that's clear and consistent.

Advertising: Beyond Word of Mouth

Mark Twain once said:

> *"Spiders spin their webs undisturbed in the doorways of merchants who do not advertise."*

I remember back when I was in sales, I used to see all these small businesses open up, stock the shelves, hire the staff, put up a big, bright sign and then stand there and wait for the customers to break down the doors.

Never happens!

The business people I saw who succeeded were the ones who were proactive, who went after new business. In Network Marketing, it's the same. The people who constantly go after new business are the ones whose checks keep getting bigger and bigger.

It's also important to reinvest your profits back into your business. And that reinvestment needs to go two places. One part goes back into those 20 percent of your people who are producing 80 percent of your group's results. The other part needs to go back into your own business-building efforts—into looking for new business-builders to bring into your business.

The most successful people in this industry put at least 20 to 30 percent back into the business on a monthly basis. That's how their garden keeps growing.

What do they reinvest in? Here are some things I've done that have worked really well.

Advertising, when done correctly, is a terrific investment. Simple ads in local newspapers can produce lots of prospects. Make the ad specific to a certain kind of person, like a doctor or an engineer. I wrote one ad that pulled beautifully with the headline:

Domestic Engineers: Earn $300 to $500 Part-Time While Spending Full-Time With Your Family.

I offered them a free information package and just gave them a voice mail number to call. Part of my message reminded them that 85 percent of all personal bankruptcies in this country could have been avoided with as little as $250 in additional income each month!

When you run ads like these, make the dollar amounts you use real and reasonable. This is true for all your prospecting, too. People have to believe the earning potential you're offering is achievable for them. "$10,000 part-time in 60 days . . ." just isn't real for most people. Here's the rule I use:

One third of their current annual income (or whatever I estimate that might be) after, say, six months to one year of part-time effort.

Here is a set of magic numbers I've heard from others in this business:

$500 to $1000 a month on a part-time basis.

Now, even little ads are expensive, because most publications reach large numbers of people. So you can cut your expenses way back by being creative and finding other ways to distribute your message.

Think about this: A seven-line ad in *USA Today* on a 10-day contract runs about $200 per day, for a total of $2,000. Now, that same two grand channeled a little differently can buy a lot of creativity—and probably produce superior results, too.

For example, how about street signs—you know, those photocopied numbers posted on telephone poles and bulletin boards around town? I did one that was great. Got a lot of response. It said:

Shed all the pounds you want without giving up the foods you love. Call this number for a recorded message and free sample.

Worked like a charm—and cost a bit less than a $2,000 ad in *USA Today*!

Another one is buttons. Now, I am not a button person. But I have to admit—buttons work! The principle is the same, no matter what form you use. I prefer a silk-screened shirt to buttons. Pop on a clever message with some neat artwork, and you'll have people coming up to you asking what your shirt's all about.

My friend Doris Wood did an amazing thing. She went to a hardware store and bought a big, crystal door knob. Then, wherever she went, she'd pull out this door knob and set it on the counter ... put it on the table beside her place setting when she was in a restaurant ... anywhere she went, she took it out and left it where it would be seen.

Now, suppose you saw this person sitting or standing there take this big crystal door knob out of her purse and place it down in front of her—are you going to ignore it,

or are you going to ask her what it's for? People asked Doris all the time.
When they did, she'd say:

"Oh, that's to remind me to let you know that the door to financial freedom is always open to you at XYZ company."

That was it. People were intrigued enough to ask Doris to tell them more—and she was off and running.

Another idea is computer bulletin boards (also called BBS's—Prodigy and America On-Line are two well-known and well-trafficked BBS's). Lots of Networkers and would-be Networkers plug into these electronic message centers. If you have a computer and a modem, just join up with one, and pop an ad on the bulletin board. They'll charge your credit card, and everybody around the country with a computer and modem who's interested in what you're offering will see your ad. Powerful stuff.

Business cards are another great resource. IT IS A MUST—get a business card from every single person with whom you come in contact. On planes, in restaurants, from retail stores and service providers you meet, get his, her or their card.

On a slow afternoon when the phone's not ringing, take out your stack of business cards and make some calls. No kidding, this works—if for no other reason than that the people you call will be so surprised and pleased you kept their card and remembered them. (And by the way, this does not work in reverse: If you expect people to whom you've given your card to take out your card when they get home and give you a call, you're in for a disappointment!)

Once, I created my own special business card which I left on the driver's side window of parked cars I passed (and I chose to leave it on expensive sports and luxury cars) which read:

"If you were absolutely certain there was a fortune in gold buried in your back yard, would you commit two years of part-time effort to dig it up? For your free treasure map, call . . ."

And then I had the phone number listed.

Regarding the phone numbers: I like to use voice mail boxes with a recorded message and an opportunity for them to leave a message of their own in response. I make sure I say in the ad that it's a recorded message or a voice mail box. That way, people are more likely to call, since they know there won't be some "salesperson" on the other end trying to sell them something.

The recorded message leverages your time, as well, and it qualifies people so that you're only following up with interested persons. You only want to talk to people that are really sincere about doing the business. You want to give them as much of the information about your opportunity as you can in a systematic way. The fact that you've got such a *system* that they can use to help them develop a supplemental income or create a full-time career really has an impact on many people.

Again, you follow up by sending them tools in the form of tapes, brochures, letters, even samples of products in some cases, along with a cover letter. Then, after giving them a couple of days to read, listen, taste, whatever—call them up and find out what interested them most in what you sent.

Another useful strategy: Send things via Priority Mail. It gets there in just two days (usually), even cross-country, and leaves a first class—no, *better*—impression, and at $3.00 per package (at the time of this writing), it's substantially cheaper than Federal Express or UPS Next Day Air.

The Great State of Taxes

Business ownership, especially small home-based business ownership, is considered by many economic experts to be the last frontier of tax relief available for the average person in North America, especially the U.S.

I won't go into the details of what deductions are available for the home-based entrepreneur. Check with your tax accountant: He or she will know better than I what specific tax breaks apply to your particular situation. However, there are some advantages that apply to just about everyone I know in Network Marketing, such as:

- AUTOMOBILES—In whole or in part, you can write off the cost of your car and all the expenses associated with it when it's involved in the business of your business.

- HOME—Some portion of your rent or mortgage is deductible as a business expense, because of your home-office and storage of product. Now, watch this one, because it might have some capital gains implications if you sell your house.

- TRAVEL—Every time you take a trip—anywhere, for any reason—if you prospect and interview or train for your business, it's a deductible business expense.

- MORE, MORE, MORE—Business equipment like computers, office and car phones, answering machines, VCRs, etc., etc., can be bought and deducted ... services, such as telephone charges, accounting and legal, even lawn-mowing (if you have meetings at the house) are deductible, too ... hire your kids to stock inventory, send faxes, clean the home-office—with some very interesting tax implications ... and more still.

Financial expert and best-selling author Charles Givens

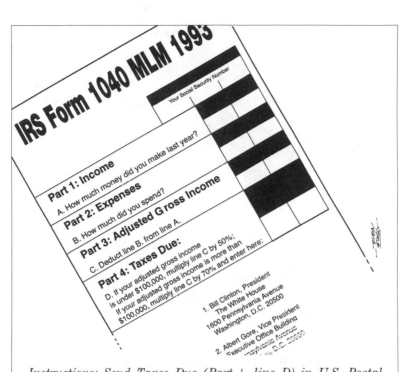

Instructions: Send Taxes Due (Part 4, line D) in U.S. Postal Money Order only! to the first name on the list; delete that person's name and add your own name to the bottom of the list. Make 10 copies of this form and mail it to 10 friends within 24 hours. In 10 days, you will personally be able to pay off the national deficit.

has a unique attitude about getting involved in Network Marketing. He advises that *everyone* have an MLM company in his or her portfolio! It's like an investment, says Givens, based on the fact that Network Marketing is one of the least expensive ways to incorporate the tax advantages of a home-based business into your financial planning. Neat idea.

His book *Wealth Without Risk* (and its sequel, *More Wealth Without Risk*) is chock-full of fantastic tax saving ideas. Get a copy, read it and refer to it often. It's very valuable.

It's About Time

There are two important things to remember about time:

One: Most people who are in this business are in it part-time; and ...

Two: There are four different time zones across the country. (And that's not even counting Hawaii and Alaska!)

Do you get what I'm driving at here? Armed with this information, you can schedule your calling times for prospecting and follow ups to hit evening hours past 6:00. Remember to always ask if this is a convenient time to talk, because you'll probably bump into somebody's dinner hour sooner or later. I try never to call new people past 10 p.m. (*their* time!) unless I know it's okay with them to do so.

Work your time zones forward or backward (depending on where you live) so that you hit people at the right times. A little schedule planning will make a big difference in completing your calls successfully.

And speaking of planning—get a daily planner. This is an absolute must! Network Marketers live or die on their ability to be and stay organized.

David Klaybor has developed a unique planner called the Powerline System, designed especially for Network Marketers. There are others—find the one that works best for you and use it religiously. I promise, it will make a big contribution to your professionalism and your success.

Party Time

The social side of Network Marketing seems to get far less attention than it deserves, in my opinion. It's been said that the most widespread degenerative disease in the world today is *loneliness*.

We live in a recognition-starved society. Why do you suppose people are always trying to be associated with their favorite sports team or watering hole? You know what they say about recognition: "Babies cry for it—and men die for it." Appreciation and recognition are values held by almost every person I know. And Network Marketing is a perfect place for experiencing and expressing those values.

Social gatherings such as pot-luck suppers, pick-up ball games in the park, beach parties, pool parties, barbecues, etc. . . . are all terrific places to show off the greatest benefit our business offers—having fun with people. Imagine inviting a prospect to a party, instead of to a meeting!

One thing people always say about their first experience with a group of Network Marketers is what incredible people we are and what fun we have together. You know why they say that? Because it's true!

I think one of the most powerful ways to introduce people to this business is to invite them to a party of distributors. Don't bother sorting or pitching them on the opportunity. Just settle back and have fun. After a couple of hours in the company of happy, successful people having a great time together, either they'll get the big picture—or they weren't the kind of people you want to work and play with in the first place.

Besides, social gatherings and parties are a must for your group. Truth is, given the choice between a party or a training, I choose the party every time. You can do more training at a party in less time, and there's not a shred of "work" about it.

Parties are great!

Trade Shows Are Super

I've also learned how to work trade shows effectively, and you can, too.

By going to the right types of trade shows—either as an exhibitor or simply as a participant, walking the floor— you can do a lot of business. Some of my best leaders and business-builders came from trade shows.

Trade shows are all about creating friendship and developing rapport with other exhibitors and attendees. I always go through trade shows having a whole lot of fun, because when you're having fun, people want to talk with you. And remember, you're always positioning yourself and your business by *who and how you are.*

One thing I do is to say to an exhibitor:

"If there were a way I could show you how you could subsidize your next trade show, would you be open and willing to take a look at the concept? I belong to a professional Network and I'd be happy to discuss how we'd be willing to split part of the cost of the next trade show with you."

Here's the question for me about the person I'm talking to: Would it be worthwhile to spend $100 to $200 if this person got involved in the business and did something, produced some results, before the next trade show? This approach gives you the opportunity to do some follow up with that person before you commit to doing a show with him or her.

If you've got your own booth, you work the show as an exhibitor, offering both your product and opportunity. I like to split the show with local distributors. Sometimes we share leads and follow ups together, but I prefer to work on their behalf—and since these are people in my organization, all my efforts with them go to building my business as well.

You don't need an elaborate booth, but there are some things I've found that work better than others. Large color pictures ... products to see, touch and try if possible ... a bunch of company tools about the opportunity and products

. . . and generic brochures, books and tapes about Network Marketing for serious prospects.

I use attention-getters all around the booth, such as gold coins (play, of course!), copies of books and tapes—anything that will attract people's attention.

A large banner with your company name, or one with an ad headline (like the one I described about having a gold mine in your backyard, or, "Domestic Engineers Earn $300 to $500 Part-Time"—depending on what kind of show it is) is a good idea. Once I made a banner with an illustration of a big rabbit wearing a Hawaiian shirt, sipping a drink while relaxing with his feet up—and a headline that read:

"I'm not on vacation; this is how I live."

We created shirts that matched the banner as well. People loved it.

Also, when you're arranging for the booth, make sure to get floodlights so your booth stands out and carpeting so you can stand up! Nothing's worse than a pair of aching feet after standing on concrete all day long. (You get these things from the exhibitor service people who help set up the booths.)

Keep it neat, professional and simple. Be enthusiastic and have fun. Remember your positioning.

Trade shows are great, because they are places where hundreds, even thousands of people *are coming to you*, rather than your going out to find them. You also get a ton-and-a-half of practice speaking with people and refining your presentation. Sure, it's intense. But once you do one and get a couple of hundred names and 10 hot prospects, it all becomes worthwhile—and *very* time-effective.

Now, I've never done this, but I've seen it work for other people: Offer a prize of some kind to attract attention to your booth. A Networker friend of mine was in line for his company's annual cruise, so he offered the trip as an incentive to the people who signed up and, with this help, he had the highest-performance month ever in the business. He got five people competing for that trip and did a heck of a volume with his new people, who all got off to a super-start. The guy who won is one of his key leaders to this day.

Be creative. Think of what would attract *your* attention—and try it out on your next show.

Which shows are best? Of course, business opportunity shows are perfect. Not only are the people coming in ready for extra income and new opportunities, but the exhibitors themselves are also usually open to hearing about anything that's new and hot. Of course, you'll have to face them trying to interest you in what they've got, but fair's fair.

Depending on your product line, consumer shows that include the kind of product you offer work well, too. The Whole Life Expo is a show held in many cities around the country that focuses on health and lifestyle products and services. I've always found them to be wide open opportunities for the kinds of diet and health products I personally favor. Other great shows are the ones geared especially for beauticians—check with your local hairstylist to find out when and where.

Other exhibitors are also a great resource for which shows are best. Many of them have been to them all and can guide you in your selection, based on years of experience. Check it out with them, just as you would ask for referrals for your product or opportunity.

And remember, everybody's looking for extra income. If you can show them a simple, effective way to earn $500 or $1000 from their own part-time business, having as much fun as you're having and using time and money-saving tools to make it easy and powerful—bingo!

Other show possibilities? There's a Working Woman's Survival Show in St. Louis, a number of franchising shows, lots and lots of health and fitness shows. You can check with major hotel sales departments or convention centers for upcoming shows of different kinds.

Barter

Barter is something I do that seems to amaze other people, and I don't know why. Barter is a very effective way to extend your Networking.

There are barter groups and Networks throughout North America, and they're a perfect way to spread the word about your opportunity, as well as a great way to experience a whole host of valuable products and services in return.

Barter is a great way of moving products and converting the people using them into new distributors.

Don't Talk Dollars

Now, I know I said that when you're running an ad, like the one I did for "Domestic Engineers Earn $300 . . ." using a dollar figure is appropriate. And I did use the example of talking about income in small, believable terms, such as $500 to $1000 a month. But the truth is, I rarely mention dollars specifically.

The reason I don't is that it's such a chancy subject. Rarely will the dollars you mention be right on target for the person you're talking to.

If you talk $5,000 to a man who's used to making more than that, he's no longer interested—even though the time freedom is something he'd love. And you can talk the same figure to a person who's never earned half that—and he or she won't believe you!

You see, it's not the money people are after—even if they *think* that's what they want. It's *what the money buys* that turns people on.

So, I always make sure I anchor what dollars people are expecting to the specific things *they want* which money will give them. I talk college education for their kids . . . a dream house by the beach . . . travel . . . free time . . . more time with their kids, their spouses, themselves. I'm always on the lookout for the "why" of the money and the "why" of getting into this business—which is different for each person.

Dollars don't inspire. Desire is what inspires.

False Expectations

One of the biggest reasons people drop out of this business is false expectations. Their "why" they got involved in the business is vital, and so is the fact that it's grounded in reality. You've got to make every effort to balance the rewards and realities of Network Marketing for people, especially in the beginning.

Just being real with people is the key. People have an instinctive ability to judge the sincerity of others.

Now, it's true that you gain the insight and ability to do this from your experience, so if you're new to Network Marketing, check with your upline to learn what expectations are grounded and which are crazy. Obviously, $60,000 a month in three months for someone who's never been in Network Marketing before is nuts!

And an interesting "problem" is that in fact, there *are* people in this business who've actually done that. But they are very few and very far between.

Besides, when you hear those kinds of numbers, get suspicious real fast. That income level in that short a time usually comes from front-loading—making money by taking it away from others—or because that person was a leader in another company, left, and brought all his or her people over to the new opportunity.

When you're first working with new people, go over the time, energy and effort they are willing to contribute to working the business, and create an income plan with them for what they can expect and when. Make it big enough to stretch for, yet realistic enough to buffer disappointment. Doing that planning together creates a solid, business-like approach that will serve all of your new distributors well in the first months, and for years to come.

If someone goes South on your program—i.e., they quit and go with another Networking company—offer to keep their existing organization alive and build it for them. Show them how they can avoid destroying what they've already built, how they can continue to reap the rewards of their previous efforts, and add even more security and residual income to their income stream.

Obviously, some people won't be willing to do this, but it's worth a try. It's the best way I know to turn a potential lose-lose into a big win-win for all involved.

Some Tips About Tools

Throughout the book, I've talked about tools. You may have the question, which tools for what person? Here's what I do. I ask them.

Now, I know there are textbooks on "modeling" and "mirroring" that can teach you how to evaluate whether the person you're speaking with is auditory, visual or whatever. I shortcut that whole business by asking them.

"Joe, would you rather listen to a tape, watch a video or read a book?"

That handles it right there. I don't have to become a neurolinguistic programming expert in order to tailor the tool to the person. Asking lets me find out which tool will be the most appropriate for that person—and it gives them the choice.

I also use tools as a barometer to determine what real interests that person has. I do this as a time saver.

Also, I always give people a time limit in which to listen, read, or watch what I've given them. Without that sense of urgency, some people will take weeks or months and still never get around to it. Of course, you don't want to waste your time with people who aren't interested, so you've got to use your judgment in the beginning. But having, say, a 24-hour time limit to view the video or listen to the cassette works well in moving people along. I simply say:

> *"Frank, I've got to have that tape back by Friday. I've promised it to someone else. Will you be able to listen to it by then?"*

Charles Possick does a wonderful thing with tools he calls a "Lending Library."

He's tested each and every tool and knows when, where and with whom they work best. He's set up a library of tools for his people to use and has his distributors sign the tools out, use them and learn for themselves which work best with their people before they commit to buying them. Then Charles gives them the ability to get the most for their investment through group buying, volume discounts, etc. It's a great system that really supports the distributors in Charles' organization.

Your Success Formula

There's a simple formula that will show you your success:

$$R = AR \ x \ ACP$$

What it means is that the "R," the Results you achieve, are equal to your "AR," your Activity Rate, times the "ACP"—Action under Correct Principles. Let's see that again:

> *Results = Activity Rate x Action under Correct Principles*

In other words, you've got to be in action—and in *right* action—to get the results.

If you are not getting the results you expect, first check your Activity Rate. You know whether or not you (or any of your people that you're managing and supporting) are in action at a rate that's appropriate. If you're not—get in action. If you are, then the problem lies in the ACP area.

Sometimes whether or not you're in Action under Correct Principles is hard to ascertain. Which principles work? Which don't? What's missing? All of these questions can be hard for beginners to answer.

Throughout this book, I've given you simple and sound principles which have worked for thousands of people and which have earned literally millions of dollars. That's a start. But if you still can't figure out what's missing in your approach, get with your sponsor or upline leader and review what you're doing. He or she will be able to provide you with the insight you need to adjust your approach, get in right action and succeed.

Show and Tell

As good as it is to have a supportive upline, here's something even better:

Become an active, supportive upline yourself!

You have tremendous power to have an impact on the success of your organization—power you may not even be aware of.

Try this exercise with your people sometime which illustrates how, as a sponsor, you are automatically a leader.

Take your thumb and forefinger and touch them together making the circular OK sign. Show this to your people and have them make the sign, too. Place the circle you've made with your fingers against your cheek. Now, move your hand down to your chin and while you do, instruct your people to make the same sign and place it against their cheek—and watch what happens.

As you look across the group, you'll find just about everyone has the sign located on their chins, just like you do. But remember, you told them to put it on their *cheeks*.

It's not *what you say* that matters. It's *what you do*.

In Show and Tell, it's the *Show* that has the power. Your people will duplicate what you show them to do by your actions. This is one of the most profound and powerful principles at work in Network Marketing.

Network Marketing is both a quality and a quantity game.

Quality is doing the right things with the right people.

Quantity is doing the above—often enough.

I'll be very straight with you: There is simply no excuse for not achieving success in this business. I mean this from the heart (and the head), IF I CAN DO IT—YOU CAN DO IT, TOO! Anybody can.

It's A Question of Balance

I read an article once that really shocked me, although now I understand what it was talking about. It said that of all the people who hit the jackpot in the quiz show, "The $64,000 Question," the great majority wound up being worse off than before they hit the jackpot. By the way, this is also true of the vast majority of lottery winners in the U.S.

Isn't that interesting? Well, you know what? I know far too many Network Marketers who hit the MLM jackpot, only to find themselves, just a few short years later, broke, in debt, and very, very unhappy people.

Balance is the key.

From the very first, you've got to balance everything about your life in this business—and the checkbook is only the beginning.

Balance the physical with the mental and emotional. This is a demanding business; you've got to use both your heart and mind, and use them vigorously. So, make sure you balance that with physical activity, diet and exercise to stay healthy and happy.

You also have to balance the *business* of this business with the *fun* of this business. Far too many Networkers, especially when they first start earning impressive incomes, throw themselves at this business so hot and heavy that the fun disappears.

I've had more fun in my years of Network Marketing, traveling, playing, finding new friends to enjoy, than I have in all the other years of my life added together. I've done that because at the start, I made fun Priority Number One. Hey, fun is why I quit my other business to do Network Marketing in the first place! Please, it's the one absolute rule I can lay down:

Find the fun—it's a must!

Balance business with family. I've seen people who've been out of balance from both sides, but most commonly it's the family side that gets the short end of the stick. One of the great joys of the "Own Your Own Life" promise of our business, for me, has been spending more time with my wife Bonnie and our children. It is truly my greatest joy. Again, it is one of the major reasons I got into Networking in the first place, so I've always made it a priority.

Again, I advise you to do the same. Life *IS* too short— much too short. Enjoy your family.

Balance is what you're offering people with Network Marketing. The opportunity to balance their personal scales of justice.

For most people—no matter if they are the founder and CEO of a corporation, a student, a household engineer or a school teacher—it's the first time in their lives someone has really made them that great an offer.

And when you do it right, when your offer really resonates with that person to the point where they have a real understanding of the possibility of Network Marketing you're offering them, it is an offer they cannot—and will not—refuse.

The Way of The Street Smart Networker

A successful Network Marketing career (either part- or full-time) requires that you be—and rewards you for being—a Street Smart Networker, a man or woman who has common sense (which isn't very common anymore) . . . who is taking action—massive action . . . and who operates under correct principles.

The road to success in Network Marketing is always under construction. Knowing the insights of the street— how distributors really think and feel, and what they need to know and do to succeed—is learned more by doing it than anything else.

There is no mystery to this business. All it really takes are street smarts.

This book is a start; now it's time to go on your own street-smarts treasure hunt. Just as I encouraged you to go out and find your own mentors, I'm sending you off with an injunction: Go seek out street smarts!

Get it from every book you can, and every tape, and every seminar. Hang out on every corner where Network Marketing wisdom is being exchanged. You can never learn enough about this business.

That's one thing I've learned and seen proven over and over again. Street Smart Networkers are hungry for learning. They've got a huge appetite for more, more, more— of everything—and it starts with a quest for learning. And because, in my opinion, Network Marketing and life operate under the exact same principles, life-learning is what you sign on for in a Network Marketing career.

Plug into that, and you will be able to live the following quote:

"We may teach what we know,
but we reproduce what we are."

And when "what you are" truly is a Street Smart Networker, and when you are reproducing that in the people you've brought into your Network Marketing business, you will experience the most richly rewarding lifestyle our world has to offer.

Be good.
No, scratch that. Be Great!

Robert Butwin

Tools I Have
Known and Loved

Books

Andrecht, Venus: *MLM Magic—How An Ordinary Person Can Build An Extraordinary Networking Business From Scratch*
Babener, Jeffrey: *Network Marketing—Window of Opportunity*
Babener, Jeffrey and Stewart, David: *The Network Marketer's Guide to Success*
Ballard, Debbi: *How to Succeed in Your Own Network Marketing Business*
Baytes, Allen: *How Secure is Your Financial Future?*
Dilley, Carol: *Tax Advantages of Home-Based Businesses*
Failla, Don: *The Basics—How to Build a Large, Successful Multi-Level Marketing Organization*
Failla, Nancy: *A Better Way to a Better Life*
—— *How to Be a Successful Self-Employed Woman*
Fogg, John Milton: *The Greatest Networker in the World*
Hedges, Burke: *Who Stole the American Dream?*
Hirsch, Peter: *Living With Passion*
Kalench, John: *Being the Best You Can Be In MLM*
—— *The Greatest Opportunity in the History of the World*
—— *17 Secrets of the Master Prospectors*
Kenyon, Stephen: *Short Cut to Easy St.*
Nadler, Beverly: *Congratulations, You Lost Your Job!*
Natiuk, Robert: *Your Destiny—Your Life and Work Become One*
—— *The Power of Inner Marketing*
Pilzer, Paul: *Should You Quit Before You're Fired?*
Schreiter, Tom ("Big Al"): *Big Al Tells All*
—— *How to Create a Recruiting Explosion*

—— *Turbo MLM*
—— *How To Build MLM Leaders for Fun & Profit*
—— *Super Prospecting: Special Offers and Quick Start Systems*
Scott, Gini Graham, Ph.D.: *Strike It Rich in Personal Selling*
Smith, D.J.: *MLM Laws in All 50 States*
Stewart, David: *Network Marketing—Action Guide for Success*
Windsor, Dennis: *Financially Free!*
—— *The Script Book*

Audio & Video

Failla, Nancy: *Financial Freedom and Prosperity*
Fogg, John Milton: *The Concept of "The People's Franchise"*
Gage, Randy: *How to Earn at Least $100,000 Per Year in Network Marketing*
Hedges, Burke: *Networking Dynamics Audio Training Program*
Myrichael Way Music: *The Sounds of Success*
Network Productions: *Turning Dreams Into Reality*
—— *Shelter From the Storm*
—— *The Blinding Paradigm*
Stewart, David: *Network Marketing in Action*
Tandem Production: *Crossroads*
Yarnell, Mark and Rene Reid: *The Ultimate Tapes on MLM*

Journals

The MLM Insider *(formerly "Downline News")* Publisher & Editor: Corey Augenstein. 330 East 63 St, Suite 7K, New York NY 10021; 800-683-DOWN (3696); (212) 355-1071.

KAAS Recruiting Newsletter Editor: Tom Schreiter. 16516 Sealark, Houston TX, 77062; (713) 280-9800.

Profit Now Editor: Chuck Huckaby. PO Box 4245, Barboursville WV 25504; (800) 229-1717.

Money Makers Monthly Publisher & President: Keith B. Laggos. 643 Executive Drive, Willowbrook IL 60521; (708) 920-1118.

Upline™ Publisher: Randolph Byrd; Editor-In-Chief: John Milton Fogg. 400 East Jefferson St, Charlottesville VA 22902; (804) 979-4427, 24-hr Voice Mail 1-800-800-6349. *Upline* also sells a series of short article reprints that look good and make a great impression. Call them for a current listing.

Other Resources

***Upline*™ Resources Catalog** *Upline's* quarterly catalog provides a large selection of the best books, tapes and other prospecting and training tools at discounts for subscribers. Most of the books and tapes listed above can be purchased through *Upline*™ *Resources*. For a free *Upline*™ *Resources* catalog call (804) 979-4427.

MLMIA (Multi-Level Marketing International Association) (714) 854-0484; FAX (714) 854-7687. The MLMIA is our industry trade group, made up of corporate, distributor and Network Marketing support members. Membership includes a host of valuable benefits and programs, and I highly recommend it. I've been actively involved in the MLMIA since I began in Network Marketing (in fact, I've twice been named "MLMIA Distributor of the Year"), and I've gotten a lot out of it.

Charles Possick (813) 392-3119. Source for mailing lists

KAAS Publishing (713) 280-9800. Source for mailing lists

Powerline System David Klaybor has created this powerful and extensive day planner system specifically for Network Marketers. An amazing tool! Available through *Upline*™ *Resources*.

Prospecting Partner® This high-tech audio tape system adapts to your phone and gives you instant access to your best prospecting and testimonial tapes so you can play snippets to someone while you're speaking on the phone. Incredible! Available through *Upline*™ *Resources*.

About Russell N. DeVan

Biography Courtesy of John Milton Fogg, Upline™ Journal

RUSS DEVAN is a successful entrepreneur, small-business owner, film producer, teacher, coach, editor, trainer, consultant and Network Marketing Sales leader. After beginning his professional career in sales and sales management with a Fortune 500 company, Mr. DeVan entered Network Marketing and quickly worked his way to Divisional Vice-President of a $60 million international consumer products company.

Russ DeVan is a million-dollar Network Marketing income-earner, one of only five presenters for the *Upline™* Masters Seminar, a Contributing Editor to the *Upline™ Journal*, and a founding partner of Success By Design—a premier Network Marketing direct sales consulting firm, one of the pioneers in the development of Network distributor satellite training. He is currently working on his first book and, in his "spare" time, has produced the surprise independent film hit *Desert Winds*.

In a profession where a person's true success is directly created and measured by the success of the others he has mentored and guided, Russ DeVan's proudest accomplishments are the constantly growing number of men and women who have achieved financial and personal freedom through their relationship with him and the power of partnership.

The Greatest Networker in the World

John Milton Fogg

U.S. $12.00
Can. $16.95
ISBN: 0-7615-1057-5
paperback / 160 pages

"John Milton Fogg will one day be recalled in the same breath as Dale Carnegie. . . . He is a top-notch motivator, and *The Greatest Networker in the World* is a modern-day classic."
—Richard Poe, author of *Wave 3* and *The Wave 3 Way to Building Your Downline*

This bestselling classic on network marketing has inspired millions to succeed in America's fastest-growing industry. It's the story of a young man on the verge of quitting the business who discovers the secrets of MLM success lie inside him. This story, from the founder and chairman of *Upline— The Journal for Network Marketing*, has changed many lives. It can change yours.

"The MLM classic."
— Richard Poe, author of the bestseller *Wave 3*

THE
Greatest
Networker
IN THE World

The story that has changed the lives of millions
Now it can change yours!

John Milton Fogg

Visit us online at www.primapublishing.com
To Order, Call 1-800-632-8676

Wave 3

The New Era in Network Marketing

Richard Poe

U.S. $14.95
Can. $19.95
ISBN: 1-55958-501-3
paperback / 288 pages

Read the book that started it all! *Wave 3: The New Era in Network Marketing* has revitalized the American dream. This book gives you the foundation you need to maximize your network marketing talents, free yourself forever from the corporate world, and utilize today's technology for building a solid, lucrative downline. This is a must-read for the must-ride Wave to recovering personal and financial freedom.

OVER 200,000 COPIES IN PRINT

Richard Poe

WAVE 3
The New Era in Network Marketing

➤ What Network Marketing Is
➤ Why It's Hotter Than Ever
➤ How You Can Ride the Wave to Financial Freedom

Foreword by Scott DeGarmo, Publisher and Editor-in-Chief of *Success* Magazine

Visit us online at www.primapublishing.com
To Order, Call 1-800-632-8676

Wave 3 Way to Building
Your Downline

Richard Poe

U.S. $14.95
Can. $22.00
ISBN: 0-7615-0439-7
paperback / 256 pages

In this companion book to the bestselling classic *Wave 3: The New Era in Network Marketing*, Richard Poe shows you how to grow your own networking empire with powerful proven strategies for quickly building a wide, deep, and lucrative downline. Redefining network marketing strategies nationwide, the Wave 3 revolution is here to stay. Don't miss your opportunity to be a part of this profitable new approach to business.

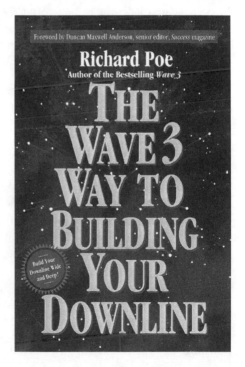

Visit us online at www.primapublishing.com
To Order, Call 1-800-632-8676

YES, for $69 I'd like
ONE FULL YEAR of the
Upline® Journal!

Name: _____

Address: _____

City: _____ State_____ ZIP _____

Phone: _____ Fax: _____

Email _____

MLM Affiliation: _____

I'd like to pay by:

❑ Credit Card. <u>**Circle one**</u>:   MasterCard   VISA   American Express

    Credit Card Number: _____

    Expiration Date:_____

    Signature:_____

❑ Check or Money Order (Enclosed)

❑ Please send me an Upline® Resources Catalog too!

NOTE: Offer valid for new subscribers only. Annual subscription is $69 for US, $79 for Canada & Mexico, and $99 for all other countries.

Credit card orders can be called into our voicemail at 800-800-6349 or to our office at 804-979-4427.

Upline®
400 East Jefferson Street
Charlottesville, Virginia 22902